HIGH COUNTRY

Walker and Company   *New York*

COUNTRY

The Rocky Mountain West

343184

Virginia Weisel Johnson

ACKNOWLEDGMENTS

Many people have contributed time, information, and encouragement in the writing of this book. I would like to thank the staffs of the Industrial Development Boards and the State Advertising Agencies of Montana, Wyoming, Idaho, Utah, Colorado, Nevada, Arizona, and New Mexico. Also, the staffs of the Missoula County Library and of the Library of the University of Montana at Missoula, Montana, as well as personnel at the Shoshone Wind River Agency in Wyoming and the Apache Agency in New Mexico. There were many individuals who helped in particular. Margit Bessenyey, while she often distracted me by luring me to competitive trail rides, more often aided by involving me in adventures in out-of-the-way places in the West that later provided source material. Mary Ruth Smith drew one of the maps.

Help in research was provided by Senator Lee Metcalf of Montana. Information was given by Mr. Jasper Ackerman, rancher-banker of Colorado Springs, Colorado; Dean Charles Bolen, Fine Arts Department, University of Montana; Mr. Thomas Paine, Political Science Department, University of Montana; Dale Johnson, Archivist, University of Montana; Ken Kautz, rancher, Bitterroot Stock Farm. Also Ronald Searle, rancher and trainer, Tucson, Arizona; Bill Crawley, Golden Sands Tour Company, Kayenta, Arizona; Roger Tsoie, ranger, Monument Valley; Wilbur West, Director of the Utah State Institute of Fine Arts, Salt Lake City, and James Hena, Tesuque Pueblo, New Mexico. Others include William Gallagher, Industrial Development Board, Sante Fe, New Mexico; Mr. Judson Moore, U. S. Forest Service, Missoula, Montana; Robert W. Young, Bureau of Indian Affairs, Albuquerque, New Mexico; Elsie Begaii, assistant employment officer, BIA, Window Rock, Arizona, and Tom Barbour, rancher, Ovando, Montana.

First published in the United States of America in 1972 by the Walker Publishing Company, Inc.

Published simultaneously in Canada by Fitzhenry & Whiteside, Limited, Toronto.

ISBN: 0-8027-0379-8

Library of Congress Catalog Card Number: 73-186181

Printed in the United States of America.

Contents

To My Husband
who has never failed me

HIGH COUNTRY

The Legendary Land

I

The rancher showing me the land he had for sale was a Mormon who had moved to Montana from Utah a few years ago. He was in his mid-fifties, wore a stocking cap on his greying head, and was a compulsive talker. Since ranching on a small acreage was no longer profitable, he worked as an upholsterer. As we tramped through the willows on the creek bottom, he told me, "I like it here but I'm moving. The winters is too cold and I got arthritis and twelve kids to feed."

"Where are you going?"

"I dunno but I'm stayin' in the West. Might not make as much money as I would if I went somewhere else, but a man's got to have room to move around."

1

The rancher stepped over a fallen cottonwood and stopped. "Now, look at that!"

We had emerged into a clearing of dun-colored grass where the creek trickled past a fringe of cattails, dried like brown paper in the late autumn. Beyond the aspen and willows, we could see great cliffs and peaks white with snow.

The rancher was not putting on an act, pretending he thought the view was spectacular so that I would be sufficiently impressed to buy the land; he genuinely appreciated the mountains. He had built his house where he could see those peaks, and he would remain in the West, in Utah or Colorado or Arizona, where he could still see mountains. I, too, had a need to see the mountains, which was why I was looking at the land, although I had little money and no prospect of being able to finance a building on the land in the future. The price for 15 acres in the 1970s was as much as my father had paid for 2,000 acres in the depression thirties. This did not matter now. I knew the rancher would sell to anyone he could, to a real estate developer or to a woodsworker who would litter the creek bottom with shacks and car bodies. That was economic reality. The man had to feed his twelve children, but he preferred that I take the land, for I would preserve it unspoiled. This was not because I was a westerner. Westerners have been the worst exploiters of the land— miners, loggers, ranchers, small businessmen who own gravel pits, gas stations, tacky housing developments. The blame for devastating the land can not be laid entirely on the big, out-of-state corporations. And people who move into the West often value the land more than those who are born and raised there. They work for conservation and zoning and up-to-date laws to protect the environment, because they have seen what has happened in other parts of the country.

Yet, exploiters and conservationists, native westerners

and new arrivals, all who live in the West or want to—what draws them to a land that can be as harsh as it is beautiful? What, in the past, had drawn my father? my grandfather? my great-grandfather? What was myth and what was the truth of this high and lonesome land?

To the average American, the West is similar to Washington, D. C., federally owned for the benefit of sightseers. And by the West, I mean the Rocky Mountain area of Montana, Idaho, Wyoming, Colorado, Nevada, Arizona, Utah, and New Mexico, isolated on one side by the Pacific coastal range and on the other by the Great Plains. The spine of these states is the Continental Divide, whose peaks notch the sky from Glacier Park on the Canadian border, south and east to the Wind River Mountains of Wyoming, down to the San Juans of Colorado, and thence to the deserts of New Mexico.

The Rocky Mountain states have—so many people believe—retained their individuality, which is another way of saying that they have lagged culturally and economically, because, today, population growth and technological development mean a diffusion of culture.

When a stranger speaks of the West, he is apt to include Texas and the Pacific coast states, which are not really western states at all. Texas, for all its high-heeled boot publicity, is a buffer between the Plains and the Deep South, while California, Washington, and Oregon have an identity of their own—particularly California, which, whatever it might be, cannot be truly defined as western. On the other hand, the eastern parts of Montana, Wyoming, Colorado, and New Mexico are included by most historians in the Great Plains. The largest amount of territory is, however, mapped as the Western Plateau and Rocky Mountain Region.

Typical of the Rocky Mountain states is the diversity of the country, which ranges from the endless, level miles of the high plains to the deserts of the Southwest and the glaciered peaks of the Continental Divide.

The region includes most of the United States that lies west of the area of twenty-inch rainfall and almost all the desert with less than ten inches of annual precipitation. Major John Wesley Powell, the one-armed soldier who understood the country as did few men, made a geological survey of the Rocky Mountain Region in 1878. In his *Report on the Lands of the Arid Region of the United States,* Powell declared that throughout the Rocky Mountain States the rainfall was insufficient for agriculture by ordinary means. The scarcity of water has been, and still is, a decisive factor. Miners and cattlemen have fought over it and homesteaders have lost their crops because of drought. Westerners are accustomed to battles, legal and otherwise, over water. During the thirties on our ranch in western Montana, a neighbor insisted he had the right to a creek that flowed through our meadow. He tore out our dam and old Charlie, who worked for us, tore out his. In the morning when Charlie irrigated, he carried a shovel over one shoulder and a rifle over the other. My Mother, I remember, was afraid Charlie would be shot by the neighbor who was similarly armed. Eventually, the quarrel was settled in our favor; none of us were surprised that the disagreement had arisen in the first place. Three decades later, the battle over the diversion of water from the Columbia Basin to the Southwest is not between individuals but between populations.

The climate is variable and given to extremes. Seldom is it mild for a long period. Recently, when we brought a number of horses from Arizona to Montana, our trucks vapor locked in the heat of the Nevada desert. The thermometer stood at 110 degrees, and we were seriously concerned about the well-being of the horses should we become stranded in the sun glaring waste where the only shade was cast by cactus and thorns. That night when we were traveling over the same desert, the thermometer plummeted 50 degrees so that we shivered with chill. Again, one winter on our ranch, the mercury dropped to 54 degrees below zero, so cold that we could hear the trees crack in the icy stillness miles away and we could not venture out of doors for fear of frosting our lungs. Every year in Montana and Wyoming unwary travelers freeze to death in the blizzards that roar down from Canada, "northers" they are called. The sudden, warm winds that follow them, melting the snow to floods, are called "chinooks."

Distances are vast in the West. One day in a Greyhound station, I saw an old man climb wearily out of a bus and ask a fellow passenger, "Where are we now?"

"In Montana."

"Montana! My God, we been driving through Montana for three days! When do we get out?"

The dominant geographic feature of the region is the mountains. The mountains affect the flow of the water, the winds, the distance between towns, the growth of crops, the raising of cattle, the people, and the people's lives.

We who live in the mountains are accustomed to them, as are the people who live on the prairies accustomed to far horizons. To the mountain dwellers, the night sounds are familiar and reassuring. Significantly, many of the people who live in isolation in the mountains are no longer young, and their way of life is passing.

Do these older people typify the real West? Or are they a relic of the past? And, above all, what is the significance of the changing West?

In the urban areas of the Rockies, people can be as alien to the West as a tourist who has never crossed the Missouri.

For them the West exists in TV serials and historical markers. They do not see the mountains from their picture windows. They are unaware of how their environment beyond their homes and offices affects their lives. A Chamber of Commerce manager not long ago declared that one of the largest Rocky Mountain states could be classified as urban. Simultaneously, the state's Supreme Court ruled for an open range. College professors and students protested Vietnam and discrimination against the Negro while, on the reservations, Indians drank themselves into insensibility to forget their poverty, as they did seventy years ago. The supermarkets are the same in Denver, Colorado, and Elko, Nevada, as they are in San Francisco or Chicago. Yet, more than eighty miles of desert separates Elko from the next large town. Tucson, Arizona, and Salt Lake City have international airports, while the largest communities of some other states are served by only one airline, and that sporadically during the winter. In Boise, Idaho, businessmen wear small-brimmed hats and carry briefcases, as do their counterparts in eastern cities; while in the wilderness areas of the same state, a couple live in a log cabin throughout the winter. A two-way radio that does not always work is their only contact with civilization, over miles of impassable drift.

All the way from the sad, blue shadows of the north to the hot, explosive colors of the south, the cowboy is waging a war of survival with the computer.

The wilderness dwellers, a Chamber of Commerce manager would say, are an illusion; the interstate highway is fact.

Today, the West is a series of contradictions, which is inevitable in periods of transition. No area in the nation has been so obscured by myth. Unveil the myth and see what the change means.

To understand the region, it is first necessary to understand the land. Do not go to the Chamber of Commerce or to the new technological and educational centers glittering with plastic and glass. The centers are superimposed on a basic structure, manmade and consequently destructible. The understanding of the West is first in the earth, second in man, and third in what man has built upon the earth.

The understanding cannot be attained on one vacation or with a crowd. The best time to see the country is in the spring or autumn after the tourists have gone, and then it is best to follow the side roads, to see out-of-the-way places, to be patient and to listen. Some people learn quickly, some over a period of years, and some never learn at all.

Those who do learn will stand among the mountains and primordial memories will wake within them. In the immense distances the present will dwindle into the past, until it will seem only yesterday that the dinosaur left his tracks in the vermillion cliffs. Once more, molten rock will boil down the sides of volcanos. The earth will shake and the wind will blow from the sand of ancient seas. In the silence a man can hear the beat of his heart echoing through the geologic ages. That beat has meant life since the Paleozoic era that lasted millions of years. Several times during the era, the sea that encompassed most of the earth invaded parts of what are now the Rocky Mountain states, and from the sea came life—the peculiar fish that, instead of dying when the tides receded, developed lungs and eventually the cerebral hemispheres that became a brain and had to be fed with oxygen to live. The scientists named this fish fresh-water Crossopterygian, and its survival was a long, agonizing process, as it stumbled from tide pool to tide pool on its stumps of fins, gulping for oxygen in the heat of blazing suns, burrowing in the slime for refuge from the whirling dust of terrestrial storms. This fish exchanged the environment of the sea for land, and, today, the blood and tears of man taste of salt from the great depths where life began.

Even before that, the mountains stirred in the womb of the earth. Miles below the surface, immense heat liquefied the rocks, gigantic pressures fractured and altered them. In following geologic periods, the sea advanced and receded over much of the Rocky Mountain region. It washed over part of Utah, New Mexico, southern Colorado, and Arizona, depositing sand, silt, and limy mud that hardened and, as the earth broke upward, lifted what had been seabed into foothills and high plateaus of shales, sand, and limestone. To this day, fossils from ancient seas can be found in the high places of the Rockies.

Immediately, after the mountains rose, there began an unceasing battle between earth forces of uplift and atmospheric forces of erosion. This occurred during an era when lateral pressures from the West folded the earth's crust into the ancestral Rockies. In the millions of years that date the next era, massive blocks of earth broke and faulted in the creation of the Rocky Mountain system. Volcanos were active, too, shaking the earth with subterranean explosions, erupting in flame and molten lava. And yet, life existed in this terror of fire and quake. Dinosaurs, birds, and mammals continued to exist when the climate cooled and ice buried parts of Montana and Idaho and glaciers formed in the peaks farther south. These alpine glaciers moved from the summits to the foothills, gouging narrow canyons into wider gorges and depositing heaps of debris at the base of the mountains. The last major mountain-making period in North America occurred shortly before the final ice age.

Geologically speaking, the Rockies are new mountains and they are still growing. At the same time, the forces of erosion wear them down imperceptibly to the untrained eye of the human whose tenure on earth is so short compared to the mountains. The rivers and storms are the most active agents. There are others, not so obvious. The rain collects in rocks that were cracked by temperature changes when the earth thrust upward. The rock particles dissolve in the humic acid in the water and in the carbon dioxide in the air. Plants, growing and decaying, form soils in which seeds are scattered by wind and birds. From the seeds grow trees that widen the cracks in the rock. A slow process? Indeed, but what is time in more than a thousand million years of geologic ages?

Everywhere in the Rockies are evidences of the immensity of time and of the violence in which the mountains were born—and man becomes aware of this as he travels the lonely roads in autumn or early spring. He might not be able to explain the feeling but he has less small talk. What he considered important is so no longer. He himself diminishes in proportion to his surroundings. In Jackson Hole in western Wyoming are peaks frequently photographed with yellow aspens fringing a lake in which are reflected the sharp, snow-etched pinnacles. The Tetons are huge Precambrian blocks, fractured and thrust upward, to be eroded by water, wind, and ice.

Drive south from Salt Lake City to Provo, Utah, where rock walls off the valley to the east. These are the Wasatch Mountains that were formed, like the Tetons, from broken blocks of the earth's crust shoved above the bed of the Great Salt Lake Basin. At the western foot of the mountains, gravel and debris have been washed onto the level. These are moraines deposited by glaciers.

In western Montana, the Bitterroots that form the Idaho border, the Madison Range, and the Beaverhead are, like the Tetons and the Wasatch, composed of uptilted blocks.

Go north again to Glacier Park on the Montana-

Canadian line to the cold, blue peaks that the Blackfoot Indians believed to be the abiding place of the gods. So titanic were the earth pressures that these mountains were shifted over the margin of the Great Plains far from their original site. Only one peak remains where the rest once were, a wedge-shaped monolith called Chief Mountain that is best seen from the alder-rimmed shores of St. Mary's at the northern entrance to the park. The forces that moved the mountains, a process called thrust faulting, originated in the Pacific Ocean as do all earth pressures in the Rockies. How can a man comprehend time older than memory? forces that moved the mountains?

In Glacier Park and in the high places of the Colorado Rockies, monstrous boulders choke the canyons and the streams, rocks that were rolled like bowling balls down the mountains by the glaciers. Here, too, it is possible to see cliffs polished smooth by the grinding ice. And in the high peaks lie emerald pools of water, incredibly clear, called paternoster lakes because they are strung like beads among the mountains. These lakes are glacial in origin, as are the shallow basins—some rock-rimmed and talus-sloped, some like alpine meadows—that the geologists call cirques.

Ice is an eroding agent. So, too, is running water, and in few places in the world is this so visible as in the Rockies where rivers have cut stupendous gorges into the mountains and plateaus. The most spectacular is, of course, the Grand Canyon of the Colorado that is over a mile deep, two hundred and seventeen miles long and, in one instance, fourteen miles across. But no figures can describe the emotion a man experiences when, after driving across the high country of Arizona, he comes abruptly upon the red and saffron terraces and the ochre-stained cliffs dropping to a river so far below that it seems no more than a thread among the rocks. Riding down the Bright Angel trail from the rim to the bottom of the canyon, a person passes through six of the Northern Hemisphere's seven botanical life zones.

Then, there is the Black Canyon of the Gunnison in western Colorado, narrow, incredibly deep, and filled with the thunder of water. And in Utah, there is Green River Canyon; in Idaho, the Snake River gorges, and in Montana, the Big Horn. Elsewhere in the Rockies, on a smaller scale, streams boil through an untold number of canyons. The cliffs are varicolored, lichen dyed, and cool and fern scented where the pools deepen beneath the rock. A characteristic, so we are told, of new mountains is the frothing rush of water.

Wind and rain erode, too—when there is rain—and this a man can see in the Painted Desert of Arizona and in Bryce and Zion Canyons in Utah, and in Monument Valley on the Utah-Arizona border, and many other places, until he can only marvel at what time and the elements have created. In Monument Valley gigantic red sandstone pillars soar a thousand feet from the desert. Bryce might be a ruined city with its towers and fluted columns and pinnacles colored in violet and sepia and cinnamon. In Zion a striped monolith rises against the hot blue sky—Moroni Mountain, so called after a Mormon archangel. Here are rocks like red sand—thin, cream-colored wafers of clay piled one on another, vermillion buttes, and lilac-shadowed mesas.

Geologists say that as the earth was thrust higher, the sedimentary blanket of rock was washed away, leaving the marvelous shapes of sandstone, conglomorate, clay, and gypsum.

How many drops of water, how many storms did it take to carve these fantasies of the West? A million years? Ten million? Look into the distance and listen to the wind.

And still there is more; the fury of volcanic eruption is

recalled in the lava beds of the Craters of the Moon in Idaho. For miles black corrugated rock has solidified in its flow. In some areas the lava is five thousand feet in depth. Livestock seldom venture there; few plants grow in the crevices. In the midst of the desolation squats a cone of cinders. Farther south near the Spanish Peaks in Colorado spread the lava beds of Raton Mesa, and in the vicinity of Mount Taylor in New Mexico stand pillars and walls of lava so hard it is difficult to chip with a hammer. The San Juan peaks in Colorado were carved out of a volcanic plateau. In Utah the Henry Mountains and Ute Peak, among others, rose molten from the earth's crust. Today, the turbulence of the geologic ages lingers in Yellowstone Park in the geysers that whoosh high into the air at regular intervals and in the bubbling mud pots and the steam that rises from vents in the rocks.

And always there are the rose-red dunes in Colorado, blown from the shores of that long-forgotten sea.

And the deserts of Nevada, like a dead world in the cold light of a waning moon. Almost all of Nevada, the western half of Utah, the southwest corner of Wyoming, and the southeast corner of Idaho lie in the Great Basin. It is an arid, hostile area of nearly 210,000 square miles with a system of interior drainage, which means that, with few exceptions, the streams do not flow out of the Basin but are sucked up by the thirsty land. The Humboldt, a brackish muddy river whose course was followed, in part, by the Forty-Niners, disappears in the stinking sloughs of the Sink not far from Carson City. The land arouses uneasiness, even in daylight driving in a car along the Interstate Highway. The hostility is everywhere, passive but implacable. All color has been burned out by the sun so that the sky is pale, the desert a dirty grey and dun. As far as the eye can see, there is only graveled flat, splotched with alkali and mountain ranges, gnawed like old bones by the wind. In the spring, shallow sheets of water spread among the greasewood and creosote bushes. Later, they evaporate to alkali that cracks like the hide of an albino beast. The Great Basin is an area where water means the difference between life and death, growth and dessication. What little rain falls is treasured, drop by drop.

The last time we drove through the Great Basin, it was at night during a rare storm with lightning flickering over the mountains and then, darkness again with only the occasional headlights of a car, and that no comfort, for peculiar things have happened to people on those lonely stretches. Terror waits in the darkness, fear in the heat of the day. Some people find a fascination in the starkness of that immense, naked land, but I am always glad to see the end of it.

A land where water is scarce, too, is the high plains country of eastern Montana, Wyoming and Colorado, where the buffalo once migrated in herds of thousands, now devoted to grazing and dry-land wheat ranches of thousands of acres. Here are the short gamma grass withered by the summer sun, eroded gullies, and wind that blows unceasingly across a thousand miles of prairie. The growing season is short and hot; in winter the northers roar down from Canada, driving cattle and sheep into drifts where they freeze with their eyes sealed shut by ice. Sometimes ranchers who go out to rescue their stock are lost in the howling, white emptiness and die within yards of the barn they cannot see. On the plateaus around Cheyenne, Wyoming, where the altitude averages five thousand feet, I have ridden day after day; the wind seldom stopped blowing, frequently attaining such force that my horse had to turn his tail against it. A favorite story was that of the wind blowing so hard and steadily that the doorbells of Cheyenne rang continuously for a week.

And, yet, there is enchantment in the high plains

country, too. What is it? Perhaps, a clarity of light and the sense of great distance.

All this a man must see when he is unhurried and there are no crowds to confuse him. Other things he may learn at any time and anyplace, mainly, how many ways the mountains dominate the West. If he approaches from the east, as did the pioneers on their trek across the plains, he will know he is reaching his destination when he glimpses the Rockies on the horizon. If he comes from the Pacific side, he will find how drastically the coastal regions differ from the high country. Crossing Donner Pass in the Sierras, he will leave the lush heat of the Sacramento Valley for the deserts of Nevada, while, farther north, Lookout Pass into Montana climbs from lowlands to the pine and rock of high elevations. In the West the climate is determined by altitude as well as distance from the Equator. Wyoming averages 6,700 feet in altitude, the northern part of Arizona comprises the Colorado plateau that is 5,000 to 7,000 feet above sea level, while in the south, the Sonora Desert is less than 3,000 feet. Parts of western Montana are hardly 3,000 feet high, and, again, in Colorado there are fifty-four peaks that are 14,000 feet or higher. In the lowlands, as in some places in Nevada and the Southwest, greasewood and sagebrush are the only plants visible for miles. Wild life in this inhospitable area is scarce, the occasional jackrabbit or coyote disappearing across the unshaded alkali. In the foothills the sagebrush continues interspersed with dwarfed cedar and piñon pine. As the foothills lift to the mountains, the land increases in fertility, or it does, if irrigated. Cottonwoods grow along the streams and jays flicker among sweet-scented alfalfa. Higher on the slopes, the leaves of quaking aspen shimmer in the sunlight, and the clear, dry air smells of pine and fir. In these woods bloom the scarlet Indian paintbrush, purple lupin, and creamy-stalked beargrass.

Deer graze in the wild meadows, and there are bears, too, and beaver to dam the streams. Climbing still higher, the pines become stunted and the grass coarsens. Lichen and green moss stain the rock and there are tiny, low-growing forget-me-nots. Here the air is cold, and from the way the grass lies, it is easy to see that the snow drifts deep into spring. Looking up, a man can see the final ascent where eagles soar among the cliffs and snow of the great peaks.

These climate zones, in many areas, are visible within a space of a few miles. At Twin Falls, Idaho, snow often whitens the ground, while, from the bridge above the Snake River, it is possible to look into the canyon and see green shrubs growing on green lawns. Again, in Arizona, the ponderosa pines and streams become hardpan and cactus where the northern plateau drops to the desert. All along the spine of the Continental Divide, the mountains form a barrier to the winds of the Great Plains. In Montana and Idaho the ranges block the storms that sweep down from the Canadian barrens. These western slopes also have more moisture, for they collect rain from the Pacific.

In the mountains originates the water that brings life to the West, the streams that flow into the three great rivers: the Colorado, the Missouri, and the Columbia.

The streams that splash down the slopes irrigate the ranches in the foothills where alluvial material was deposited by the glaciers. This outwash of silt and gravel built up into parks between the ranges and into moraines far out on the western and eastern flanks of the Divide. But the land is not particularly rich for farming. The topsoil is too thin and spotty, making it best suited for livestock. Much of the land in the West is submarginal, that is, it produces below normal. Perhaps the best that can be said is that there is so much land. The Rocky Mountain states extend over a thousand miles from Canada to Mexico. The Southwest is larger than New York and New Jersey and all six New England states plus Pennsylvania and Ohio. Utah approximates the size of Great Britain, while Montana is the third largest state in the continental limits.

These things a man must keep in mind while he journeys across the West. Above all, he will remember that primordial fear stirred by the solitude of man in the geologic ages. Man has grown accustomed to thinking of himself as the center of the universe. Indeed, he has defined the universe. Yet he sensed that we are lost in the immensity of time and violence that created the earth. Seamen on night watches often share this disquiet. So, too, do pilots flying a solitary way through the skies, and, it is said, so do those who die slowly and alone in the grey morning hours.

This, then, is the land.

The People Who Created the Legend

II

Because of its remoteness and its aridity, the population of the Rocky Mountain area lagged behind other parts of the nation. The first westward migration passed over the Rockies to Oregon and the California gold fields; when gold was discovered in Colorado, Idaho, and Montana in the sixties, the region gained in population, only to experience a lag again after 1920. World War II saw another population growth in the region, and, while the northern Rocky Mountain states have not gained as rapidly as those in the Southwest, great changes have occurred throughout the area, which have affected the economy, the culture, and the society of the people who live there.

Phoenix has become the Los Angeles of Arizona, while Tucson, Arizona, has developed an urban sprawl of seventy-two square miles. Tucson could serve as an example of what has happened. During the 1950s it had a fantastic growth—from 45,000 people to more than 236,000 in 1960. The growth continued throughout the sixties. In 1965 it was estimated that 1,500 new residents a month had moved into the Tucson area.

"Cosmopolitanism without protocol," the boosters declared proudly, "sophistication without pretensions."

These slogans mean that new housing developments have swallowed the old Mexican adobes and that real estate promoters are platting the desert where nothing grows but cactus.

General William T. Sherman of Civil War fame would be amazed if he could see Tucson. In 1880 when he visited Arizona with the presidential party of Rutherford B. Hayes, he exclaimed, "What a hell of a country!"

To this, an Arizona host replied, "Why, General, it is not such a bad country. . . . Possibly Arizona is a little bit warm but all she needs is more water and better immigration."

Sherman snorted, "That's all hell needs!"

Salt Lake City, Utah, and Denver, Colorado, have become manufacturing and transportation centers, and Albuquerque, New Mexico, boasts a prosperity that the most optimistic Chamber of Commerce official would have hesitated to predict before World War II. These cities, among a number of others in the Rocky Mountain region, have become metropolitan statistical areas. This means they are similar to other cities in many respects, but cannot be considered as urban as New York or Chicago, whose populations run into the millions. The mountains in Tucson and Salt Lake City are close, and it only takes a short time to drive to open country from Albuquerque or Denver. This can be disappointing for the few people who hope for the big-city atmosphere, such as the woman from Dallas, whom I met at a Taco Drive Inn—a chain that is replacing the old, family-owned Mexican restaurants in Tucson.

"Boy, I'll sure be glad to get back to Dallas!" the woman confided over a bowl of chili. "In Tucson you drive a few minutes and you're out of town, and then where do you go? In Dallas you can drive for three hours and never get out of the city."

The population of the Rocky Mountain West has become statistically urban, and the people who moved into the cities have developed a uniformity. Only a few old-timers who scowl at the bulldozers and the increased taxes for schools retain their identity—and they don't matter. The entrepreneurs have usurped their economic and social position.

The modern emigrants who come from within the state or more distant parts of the country cannot be called pioneers. They have arrived by automobile or plane, and their greatest hardships have been finding a house in which to live and adjusting to a new job. On the whole, they are better educated and more financially secure than the emigrants who moved west in a covered wagon. The religious faith that sustained the women in sunbonnets is of little importance, as are the norms of social behavior that characterized the first westward movements. People have become more informal. Slacks are the universal costume; bright-colored synthetic materials are worn in the south; jeans and warmer synthetics in the north. Dyed hair, eye make-up, and accessories are common everywhere. Fads reach Denver a few months after New York, as much as six months or a year late in Great Falls, Montana. Automobiles have become the accepted mode of transportation, so much so that there are no sidewalks in the new parts of the cities and few means of public conveyance.

No one seems to have been born in the area in which he lives, particularly in the Southwest. I talked to a horse trainer in Tucson who came from Wisconsin. When I asked him if he missed his old home, he exclaimed he wouldn't go back to such a cold climate for anything; he was "sold" on the dryness and sunshine of the desert. A gas station lessee told me he was a retired army captain who had been stationed in Arizona during World War II, liked it, and came back because the Southwest offered better living and job opportunities than his small home town in the Midwest.

"Although," he hastened to add, "jobs aren't that easy to find around here."

A retired, middle-aged couple, whom I met at a horse show, had moved to a retirement center because the husband had asthma. A wife, whose husband was employed in one of the new electronic industries that recruit promising college graduates in other parts of the country, worked in an office at Sandia Air Base in Albuquerque.

There are thousands of similar couples employed in industries and defense installations and research laboratories that have located in the Rocky Mountain area since World War II. The black population has increased, also, in urban centers such as Denver and Phoenix, but nowhere near to such an extent as on the Pacific coast. In the Southwest, the Mexicans provide a low cost, nonunion labor force, and in states such as Montana, Idaho, and Wyoming that are predominately rural and where agriculture and mining are the mainstays of the economy in many areas, there are no jobs to attract a black migration. What few blacks there are, seem to center around the universities in the north.

State Employment Commissions report increases in letters from people who, ignorant of statistics, want to move from heavily urbanized areas in other states to a sparsely populated region, which the Rocky Mountain West remains, despite its amazing growth. People write that they are afraid of urban riots, or they want a simple life where there is no smog or congestion, or they'd like a change in climate, or they believe a certain area is booming. The greatest number of letters come from California, Illinois, Michigan, Wisconsin, New Jersey, New York, Pennsylvania, Texas, and Ohio. New Mexico's Job Service Director said in 1969 that people "want more opportunity that they believe is in the West."

"Go West, young man, go West!" thundered Horace Greeley—over one hundred years ago, crusading editor of the *New York Tribune*, abolitionist, and proponent of the agrarian utopia. Generations of men and women followed his advice. The frontier became synonymous with opportunity.

Like all myths, that of the frontier is subject to examination. What I'd call the last of the geographic frontier lingered until the outbreak of World War II. In terms of personal experience, this meant being snowed in during winter months on a ranch where we cooked on a wooden range and read at night by lamplight because we had no electricity. It meant driving over narrow, graveled roads that could be blocked by snow or turned into a morass of gumbo by rain. It meant shopping at locally owned grocery stores in small towns and seeing elk and deer in the ranch meadows. Land was cheap and so were cattle. Wages were low and jobs were scarce. The Indians still wore their old buckskin costumes and danced for their own enjoyment, and if the battery ran down in the radio, we had no news for days.

People did not move around as much as they do now. Life had become static. The daring and the vitality of the early days had withered in the harshness of economic survival. The West that had been young had grown old.

If the frontier meant opportunity, the Rocky Mountain region had failed to fit this definition for many years. The most popular and widespread hypothesis in the nineteenth century contended that the frontier was the boundary between savagery and civilization, and civilization was personified by the yeoman farmer. It also contended that the existence of an area of free land, its continuous recession, and the advance of American settlement westward explained American development. Settlement was a struggle of man against nature, which was a major factor in the creation of democracy. Our economy, our politics, and our national characteristics were influenced by the land-man ratio. This theory of geographical determinism, popular in eighteenth-century England and France, was endorsed by Presidents Jefferson and Jackson. Later, it was enlarged upon by intellectuals and by Horace Greeley, who preached that the ideal was a nation of yeoman tilling their own land and that the availability of free land alleviated poverty and unemployment and the exploitation of labor.

This theory would be interesting to the recent emigrants to Arizona, where, in 1968, nonfarm jobs accounted for over 93 percent of employment in the state.

Critics of the agrarian utopia felt that the frontier was defined too narrowly by theory: geographical limits could not be put on the frontier, and there were other possibilities for man's hopes and ambitions than just the physical. Also, the agrarian utopia did not take into account the Industrial Revolution or mining or the growth of cities. In addition, it tended toward idealism. Indeed, one of its leading proponents described the transcontinental migration as a westward-marching army of individualistic, liberty-loving, democratic backswoodsmen.

What cannot be argued is that the American West, popularly known as the frontier, led to the creation of one of the world's great myths. What is more, it became a myth in its own time, propagated partly by those who benefited financially or politically, and partly by well-meaning intellectuals. It caused untold heartbreak, defeat, success beyond men's wildest dreams, and personal fulfillment that had nothing to do with worldly goods. Amazingly, the myth still exists.

Before we assess the present-day emigrant, we must learn something about the pioneer who created this myth. What was he like, the westerner of the early trans-Mississippi migrations? It would be interesting to know if he developed characteristics on the frontier, if these characteristics remain today in the changing West, and if these traits conflict with those of the modern emigrant. To be fair, the pioneer should be judged according to his time in history and always with an understanding of the geographical aspects of the Rocky Mountain region—which we shall call the last of the great frontier.

What becomes immediately apparent is that the frontier was a recent experience. Many of the characters of western myth lived to modern times. Mrs. George Armstrong Custer listened to the re-enactment of the battle of the Little Big Horn on the radio; when it was over, she turned to my friend John Hutchins and said, "That's the way it must have been." As a child, I met Granville Stuart who discovered gold in Montana. He attended a meeting of the Montana Pioneers at our home, and I remember him as a handsome man with a white beard, much respected, which led me to confuse him with God. My own great-grandfather, while not an historical figure, came west in a gold rush. Even in his eighties, he was vital and aggressive. Like numbers of his contemporaries, he liked his liquor and was possessed by a spirit of restlessness. Every winter he went to California, which was the farthest

west he could go in America. The family thought he was looking for warm weather. Now, I wonder if he was still not
searching for a frontier.

Men like my great-grandfather and Granville Stuart
typified their environment. While not yeomen farmers, they
lived close to the land, and their skills and much of what they
thought and said and did was influenced by the mountains
and the plains. The present-day emigrant is employed in
manufacturing and service and government jobs, and has little contact with his natural environment.

The most enduring of the western myths was gold, first
symbolized by the Conquistadores, who were drawn to the
then unexplored region of the Southwest by tales of turquoise
and tinkling bells of precious metal. Like a mirage, these six-
teenth-century Spaniards marched across the deserts of the
Southwest, the sun glinting on armor, pennants fluttering
from lances, and, in their train, the priests carrying the cross
to the Indians. When the Conquistadores failed to find treasure, they turned back, leaving behind the hostility of the
Apaches, as well as the distrust of the Pueblo people who wa-
tered their crops by intricate systems of irrigation, and who
had highly developed crafts and a religion that was, in some
ways, more spiritual than that of the priests who sought to
convert them. Also, the Conquistadores left behind the scarlet and yellow flag of Spain to claim what is now New Mexico,
Arizona, California, and parts of Colorado, Utah, and Nevada.

Thus the Spanish influence was established in the Southwest. Later it was diluted by Mexican-Indian customs, and,
despite annexation by the United States of this area after the
Mexican War of 1848 and the subsequent treaty of Guada-
lupe-Hidalgo that pushed Mexico south of the Rio Grande,
the culture remained predominant for many years. Anchored

on the Catholic Church, it was passive rather than aggressive, and it blended with the land. To the West, it gave the stock saddle, chaps, the broad-brimmed hat, the adobe house, and chili—artifacts that, in addition to being practical, happily lend themselves to commercialization, which is the reason they have endured. Even the Conquistadores have proved profitable as murals in countless bars in Arizona and New Mexico. And the myth of gold still exists in the legends of lost mines, largely due to the advertisements in western magazines for metal detectors and fourwheel-drive vehicles.

To the Southwest credit must be given for recognizing that profit is the biggest incentive to the perpetuation of myth. The discovery, however, is recent. The early emigrants who pushed west over the Santa Fe Trail were not charmed—as were later-day tourists—with the alien customs they found in Tucson and Santa Fe. Many of these emigrants were a far from idealistic type of backwoodsman—uneducated, impatient of aliens in territory they considered theirs by conquest. The myth that the pioneers were racially tolerant was a figment of the imagination of romantic novelists. To the pioneer, the Mexicans were "greasers." The Chinese, who were brought in to work on the railroads and remained to mine the gold camps, were called "Chinks," and the Indians were "bloodthirsty savages." The blacks, who were few in number, were regarded with equal contempt.

Today, people in the Rocky Mountain area like to think of themselves as racially tolerant, which is easy because the tolerance is mostly theory. Black migration has not increased to any appreciable extent in the region, and the Indians are either on reservations or too few in number in the cities to be noticed. The Chinese have virtually disappeared, and the Mexican is becoming Americanized to the extent that he is losing his identity. If these minority groups became an economic threat or grew militant, the situation might be different.

Ironically, the early-day emigrants, or their fathers, who were noted for their intolerance, had at one time been aliens themselves in a strange land. The first were largely Protestant North Europeans who moved to the Alleghenies, through the Cumberland Gap, on to Kentucky, Illinois, and Wisconsin. Some of them remained there but others were not satisfied. Across the Mississippi lay a wider, wealthier land with mountains such as few men had beheld and rivers running to the western sea. All these people needed was an incentive to move again. A characteristic, we are told, of a frontier is the mobility of its population. If this is so, the West is still a frontier in that respect, and it would seem that myth still sparks the mobility. Western myth was founded on hope; opportunity was always on the other side of the mountain. Hope is a greater incentive to effort than despair, and so we find the same myth, modified by the late-twentieth century, inspiring migration that motivated it one hundred years ago.

Public relations men would do well to study the explorers for pointers on how to enlarge upon the myth. Captains Meriwether Lewis and William Clark—who explored the region of the upper Missouri in 1804-1806 that included what is presently Montana, Idaho, and Oregon—kept a detailed journal. While the expedition was remarkable for its efficiency and its contribution to scientific knowledge, what impressed the average person was the report of so much free land—that and the human interest stories of grizzly bears and Sacajawea, the Indian woman guide. Lieutenant Pike, who explored the southern Rockies and for whom Pike's Peak is named, introduced an element of suspense when he was taken into custody by the Mexicans who still controlled the Southwest at the time; but the greatest contributor to the western myth was John Charles Frémont. Where the other explorers stuck to dry fact, Frémont grew ecstatic, for he was a romantic who believed in national expansion.

This, we must remember, was the age of Manifest Destiny in America and of the Empire in Europe when colonialism was the white man's obligation, not his crime.

Once planted, the seed of western myth was cultivated by politicians who hoped for the support of new states in their growing differences between North and South and by financial and business interests as well as western land speculators who hoped to benefit from the settlement of the frontier.

Frémont not only glamorized the country, he glamorized the inhabitants as well, although, at the time (the 1840s), these were remarkably few in number—Mexicans in the Southwest, Indians everywhere else, and a handful of trappers.

The trapper, or mountain man, is still a popular figure, bearded and wearing fringed buckskins. In the 1930s men still lived who might have been called mountain men. We knew one in western Montana who snowshoed into the wilderness area every winter to run a trap line. The financial returns were small, and it demanded moral as well as physical stamina to endure the cold, the hard labor, and, above all, the loneliness. A stranger meeting our friend for the first time would have noted only an old man who talked very little.

Our friend did not resemble the so-called mountain man or hermit to whom we were introduced last summer in the Salmon River country. The "hermit" was famous, articles had been written about him, and we were told we must not miss him on our float trip down the turbulent stream that cuts deep into the mountains of central Idaho. As it turned out, we couldn't have missed the hermit; he was waiting on the beach to take us to his cabin to tell us about his life and how he made his clothes from animal skins and his cooking utensils and guns from scrap metal. Dressed for the part, the hermit wore a beard, a fringed shirt and a Conquistador-like helmet of stitched leather. As we followed him up the path, one of our party whispered, "Note the helmet. It comes in a Tandy leather kit."

We might ask what was the appeal of the mountain man, and the explanation would be—the same as the cowboy; a trapper was an adventurer with whom a man could identify. Actually, the trapper was not as heroic a figure as he was depicted in epic poems and novels. He was supposed to be independent and heedless of pecuniary reward, and he pursued his dangerous way because of his love of the wilderness. This was not strictly true. Most trappers signed up for the fur trade because they needed a job, and the fur trade offered a chance for wealth and excitement. Few of them started into the mountains alone; they were hired or financed by fur companies, and these companies were highly organized, competitive, and dependent on eastern markets for the prices received for their furs. The majority of trappers had Indian wives or paramours; they traded with the Indians and frequently lived in their camps, but they still considered the Indians treacherous and cruel. If one of their companions was killed by Indians, they reacted with ferocity. But worse than the killing of individual red men was the introduction by the trappers of liquor in the trade for buffalo robes and furs, thus initiating the degradation of the western tribes. In addition, the trappers brought venereal disease and smallpox that decimated entire nations. The traditions and amenities of civilization that did not contribute to survival were scorned. Whoring, drinking, and exploitation of wild game were also part of the mountain man's character. By the 1850s the trappers had nearly exterminated the beaver from streams where they had once been plentiful. Indeed, they set a pattern of exploitation in the Rocky Mountains that was to exist to the present day.

The only aspect of the trapper's life that has not been exaggerated was the danger. Accidents, grizzlies, and Indians presented hazards enough but the greatest peril lay in the land itself—the deepening snow when game became scarce, threatening starvation; the blizzards that rose on a long, empty cry of the wind; the rivers that, in the spring, overflowed their banks so that a man might drown. In the Southwest the dry arroyos could, without warning, crest with a roaring torrent that swept everything before it. Then, there were the deserts—the Sonora and the Mojave and the Great Basin. Jedediah Smith, one of the best known trappers, returning from California, crossed the Great Basin; he and his companions nearly died of thirst in that arid waste, where dust devils gyrated across the alkali, and the peaks jutted like teeth from shrunken gums of sand.

John Work, a partisan of the Hudson Bay Company in 1831, listed his engagés. "Cloutier, killed by Blackfeet . . . Dumais, drowned in Snake River . . . Letandre, killed by Blackfeet . . . Wm. Raymond, mortally wounded . . . Rondeau, taken sick . . . Soteaux, missing . . . Probably died in the mts . . ."

What remains unique about the trappers was that they walked a wilderness that had not been seen by white men since the dawn of time. That cannot be magnified by myth.

If men could identify with the trapper, women were better able to identify with the emigrant in the covered wagons whose turning wheels signified the end of the fur trade. Women, who are more practical than men, were not susceptible to the myth of freedom and adventure in the wilderness. The trapper remained a masculine myth, and it is significant that, beyond the obvious reasons, white women did not accompany the fur brigades into the mountains. Not until a home, church, schools, and security were added to the western myth did women cross the Missouri in any numbers. They did not want to.

The emigrants were as human as the trappers. Francis Parkman, the young Bostonian and chronicler of the Oregon Trail, wrote in 1846 that the emigrants were rude and intrusive and some of the men typified the "raw, noisy, western way." "They lacked discipline, and, in their camps, there was confusion with the women crying and the men quarreling. What was more, in one emigrant train, the women were 'damned ugly.' "

The women, for their part, scorned the trappers that Parkman admired because they grunted like grizzly bears and shared a tipi with a "squaw" and a brood of half-breed kids. Not only did the women resent the outraging of their Victorian morals, but they resented American men finding satisfaction with women of another race.

The Indians terrified the women, too, and rightly so. The members of the Hardinbrook wagon train, so called because it was captained by my great-grandfather, saw what had happened to an emigrant party just ahead of them—the still smouldering wagons, the horses gone, and the piles of stones marking the graves. Unlike Parkman, the women had scant sympathy with the "peaceful" Indians, most of them agreeing with Sara Raymond, the narrator of the Hardinbrook expedition, who wrote: "I fail as yet to recognize the 'noble red man.' They are anything else than dignified; they seem lazy, dirty, obnoxious-looking creatures." To Sara Raymond, who was young and pretty, the westward journey was a picnic, so her criticism was not based on the intolerance of an older generation.

Today we can see that Sara was thoughtless and that

Parkman was a snob. Parkman could not understand that the men in homespun were creating a nation but not, it must be understood, from patriotic motives, although patriotism was ascribed to them later. In 1849 a nugget had been found at Sutter's Mill in the Sierras, and ever since, the western sunset has been tinged with gold. This was fact, not the illusion that had misled the Conquistadores. The fact, enlarged on, distorted by rumor, grew to the greatest myth the West has ever experienced.

Grandpa Hardinbrook had the gold fever, and Sara Raymond's two brothers hoped to recoup the family fortunes in the placers of Montana, an ambition that the pious Sara felt was not what it should be. To volunteer as a missionary, she felt, was sublime, but to pull up stakes and leave all that made life worthwhile, to start on a long, tedious and dangerous journey to seek a home among strangers with no other motive than gaining wealth was not wholly admirable. The motive did not seem to justify the inconvenience, the anxiety, the suspense that had to be endured. "Yet how would the great West be peopled were it not so?"

Sara, because of her youth, could be allowed such sentiments. Her mother well knew why she had brought the family west.

Seldom has the world seen such a heterogeneous multitude. Sara described camping on the Platte with two hundred wagons in sight and marveled at what a great number of people were going west that spring. Farther south on the Santa Fe trail, the scene was repeated. A trader listed in his party a tailor, a silversmith, a German peddler, a talkative Frenchman, two Germans who hardly talked at all, two "eccentric" Polish exiles, voluble Mexicans, and American backwoodsmen. My great-grandfather was a doctor, Sara Raymond's mother was an educated widow. Others were lawyers, newspapermen, drifters, entrepreneurs, the ill in search of health, remittance men, confidence men, ex-Confederates (after the Civil War), Mormons, New England rock farmers, missionaries, poor whites from the border states, eccentrics, criminals, and Englishmen.

They traveled by any means they could, by wagon drawn by oxen or mules, by horseback, on foot, in carryalls, or pushing hand carts. With them they carried their worldly goods and frequently their pets, such as dogs, canaries, and cats.

Some were inspired by myths other than gold—free land, a lucrative trade, better opportunity in a profession, release from debt, founding of religious colonies free from persecution. Of those attracted by the last motive, the Mormons predominated, and their journey to Utah of more than 20,000 men, women, and children, over a period of several years, was led by Brigham Young, an inspiring leader for his devoted followers. A stocky, dedicated, and determined man, Brigham Young organized the Saints into a cohesive unit and inspired and thundered at the weary pilgrims until he got them, including several thousand English and Swedish emigrants pushing hand carts, across the plains to what became the capital of Zion, Salt Lake City.

As a little girl, I believed that Mormons had cloven-hoofs, because I had heard how Grandpa Hardinbrook—who, when he was not gold mining or doctoring, had operated a freight line between Corinne, Utah, and Virginia City, Montana—had been chased out of Corinne by the Mormons. Not until I was grown did I realize that the hostility of the Gentiles was (and I might say, still is) based on the economic expansionist policy of the Church of Latter-day Saints. On the frontier polygamy was anathema to devout Protestants (Brigham Young had twenty-nine wives), but what was even worse was the belief of the Saints that they would inherit the earth financially, and because of hard work and united effort, they often did, or, at least, parts of it. Indeed, economics had been the basic cause of their persecution in the east, from whence they had been driven across the plains. In the twentieth century men shrug and say, "The Mormons are buying up everything."

For the emigrants who were well prepared, the journey was fraught with peril; for those who lacked the money or sense to outfit themselves well, the trip was often disastrous. The temperate landscape of northern Europe and the eastern part of the United States did not prepare them for the hostile deserts and mountains of the west. William Kelly, an Englishman, told how wagons sank hub-deep in the sand, how the dust inflamed men's eyes, and how their lips caked into open sores. Axles broke on the wagons, cattle stampeded, thirst tortured people with mirage. When they did find water in areas like the Great Basin, it was too bitter with alkali to drink or contaminated by the putrefying carcass of an ox. Swollen rivers had to be forded, storms erupted with rain and lightning, drenching families whose only shelter was beneath the wagons. The wet canvas of the prairie schooners flapped dismally in the wind; the blankets were wet, and the women went about their chores in rain-soaked shirts. At the end of the day, children were tired, cross, and often sick. Someplaces, there was not enough grass for the animals. Other wagon trains ran short of supplies and the people weakened with starvation. Or they were caught by cold weather and stalled in deep snows, where their feet froze—which often meant gangrene—and they were forced to eat their own animals. Some, exhausted, went mad. Worst of all was illness —dysentery and cholera and mountain fever. My great-grandmother had mountain fever, and her greatest fear was that one of her loved ones would die and be buried on the plains, which was a desecration because of the lack of coffins and the wolves that dug up the bodies.

Fatigue irritated tempers. Quarrels disrupted wagon trains. "So many are poor, so many ignorant, so many are foolish," wrote an emigrant of the times.

The trail was littered with the debris of overloaded and broken wagons, trunks of clothes, ploughs, stoves, dishes, dead animals, graves.

"We passed eight graves on the mountain," Sara Raymond wrote and two days later, "We passed a grave this morning that was made yesterday for a young mother and her new-born babe."

An untold number turned back before they reached the mountains. Others returned to the States when their quick-rich dreams did not materialize.

"We have been meeting men all day returning from the mines," Sara wrote. "They give a doleful account of the hard times in Montana."

But the members of the Hardinbrook wagon train could not believe that they would not be among the fortunate ones, and so they continued their journey to Alder Gulch.

More than a century later, we stopped at a combination bar and café in northeastern New Mexico, which is high plateau country where dirt roads branch off across empty, wind-swept space. The bar, like the town, was dated in the 1880s. The ceiling was patterned in molded tin squares, and the mahogany bar was backed by a mirror framed in massive pillars of the same wood. The bartender, who doubled as cook in a greasy apron, served us pinto beans and tacos, talking all the while.

"You passing through?"

We said we were, and the bartender said it was a lot easier traveling on the new highway. "The Santa Fe trail used to run just east of town. Someplaces, you can still see the ruts."

Our companions on our trip were two Mormons wearing high-heeled boots and big hats, and the discussion centered on how difficult it must have been to cross the plains in a wagon.

"Folks wouldn't stand what the pioneers did," one Mormon said.

"That's for sure," the bartender agreed. "They'll come out here for a new job or because they like the country but they'll only come if it ain't too much effort."

"Why?" I said. "Why won't people stand hardship any more?"

The bartender and one of the Mormons shook their heads. The other Mormon thought awhile, and then he said, "I guess it's because people don't believe in things the way they used to."

The Riches
of the Earth

III

In the high, arid mountains of southwestern New Mexico is the Santa Rita copper mine, an open-pit operation gouged from the belly of the mountain. Standing on the rim, we looked down on a series of immense terraces colored greyish blue, saffron, turquoise, and cinnamon. The pit was over a thousand feet deep and a mile and a quarter across. Gigantic shovels gulped tons of earth, swinging their loads into waiting trucks. The roar of equipment beat on our ears. Occasionally, a blast echoed across the crater. The pit was being enlarged and what the engineers called overburden was being removed —thousands of tons of sedimentary rock and volcanic tuff that had buried the magma that seventy million years ago had boiled from the earth's core to fill the cracks of rock with copper, iron, and sulphur.

The Santa Rita Mine is operated by the Kinnecott Copper Corporation, which also operates the open-pit mine near Bingham, Utah. The Utah Mine produced 18 percent of the copper in the United States in 1962. In Nevada we had seen other copper operations, as well as the Anaconda's open Berkely pit in Butte, Montana, and the Lavender pit near Bisbee, Arizona, the latter of which has an estimated 41 million tons of copper ore. Millions of dollars in copper have been taken from these mines. More millions have been made in mines that produced gold, silver, manganese, molybdenum, uranium, nonmetallic metals, oil, and natural gas.

In the popular imagination, the West is synonymous with gold and silver. Myth has encouraged us to believe that a poor man, by chance, can stumble on a fortune. Therefore, it is apt to be a shock to learn that very little gold and silver is mined in the West today and that what is produced is largely a by-product from mines whose output is concerned with other metals. Mining has decreased in importance in every state in the Rocky Mountain West, and if petroleum, natural gas, sand, and gravel were not listed in the states' mineral output, the decline would be drastic, indeed. In Arizona the 1968 output of sand and gravel—reflecting the construction expansion—was valued at more than $21 million while that of gold was valued at little more than $3 million. In New Mexico in 1967, petroleum production was valued in the millions of dollars while gold ranked much lower, and was then described as having been recovered from other ores. In Colorado the emphasis is on minerals the early-day prospectors never heard of, such as molybdenum, vanadium, and tungsten, although much of the value of total mineral output comes from petroleum, coal, and related products. In Wyoming, which lists mining its most important industry, nearly 85 percent of the annual mineral output is attributed to oil, natural gas, and coal.

Driving through the West, you see oil wells pumping among the sagebrush hills. The country is usually barren, arid, and uninhabited, and it is disconcerting to see the rigs, like large blackbirds, dipping their beaks, rising back, dipping again in a monotonous, endless rhythm. Salt Creek in Wyoming, which has been in production since 1908, was one of the first fields in the Rocky Mountain area. Years before it was discovered, cowboys riding the range saw a sloe-colored, odorous seep on the cracked earth, but they had no idea of the wealth it signified, and at that time, western oil reserves did not have the economic importance they were to assume later.

More than one rancher flies his own plane to Acapulco in the winter because oil was discovered on his land, although these men are not in the same income bracket as the Texan we met at a Colorado horse show who drove a white Cadillac and owned the world's champion cutting mare. When I observed that he must own a few oil wells to afford the mare, he took his cigar from his mouth and said, "Ah don't own oil wells, Ah own oil fields!"

While gold and silver have experienced a decline, copper is still listed as one of the most important minerals in the West. The Utah Mine, for instance, is advertised as the largest open-pit copper mine in the world. I don't know if this is true, since Americans, particularly westerners, like to proclaim universal supremacy. The Santa Rita Mine is described as the most beautiful. Actually, it is the oldest copper mine in the Rockies, for it was worked by the Spanish who forced Indian slaves to dig the ore in narrow, underground shafts and to carry it to the surface on their backs. The overseers did not spare the whip and cave-ins were frequent. For the cruelty of the Spaniards, the Apaches retaliated by ambush and raids; contemporary accounts tell us that their arrows were tipped with copper.

It could be that the golden bells of Gran Quivera, which led the explorer Coronado to his fruitless quest on the plains, were of copper from Santa Rita. Before the white man came, the Indians mined outcroppings that needed no smelting and fashioned them into ornaments that have been discovered in southwestern ruins.

The supply of pure copper in Santa Rita and in the other mines in Montana, Arizona, and Utah was limited. Myth has led us to believe that the discovery of western minerals—so pure they only had to be dug out with a shovel—resulted in national prosperity. While this claim is tantalizing, it has been exaggerated. Copper is an example. As early as 1860, mining men in the West wanted to develop copper reserves, but until the 1880s, the supply of the metal from Michigan was adequate. In 1880 when the electric industry began to expand, the demand for copper increased so that it became economically feasible to exploit the western ores. Newly constructed railroads made the copper-rich areas accessible. Equally important was the development of new mining and smelting methods. The high-grade ore that assayed as much as 20 percent copper a ton was not difficult to mine and needed only simple concentration, but within a few years the high-grade ore was exhausted, leaving the deeper sulphide ore that averaged less than 6 percent copper and, eventually, as low as 0.75 percent. The mines might have been abandoned if the challenge had not been met by the invention of better explosives, and more efficient drilling, hoisting, mechanized pumping, and, in smelting, the oil flotation method of concentration which made it possible to recover a greater amount of copper from the ore than in the past.

Thus the western minerals, with the exception of placer gold, depended on national markets and the inventive genius of engineers to be profitable, and then the money flowed, not to the bearded prospector of myth but to a corporation.

Today, a Holiday Inn provides a swimming pool and air conditioning to the traveler in Silver City, the nearest town to Santa Rita, and the men in heavy-soled boots and dusty trousers prove to be real estate promoters, not miners. But if you stand quietly among the dry, broken hills stubbled with piñon, you can feel the ghosts gathering in the twilight.

As I watched the jaws of a big shovel slaver above the ground at Santa Rita, I thought of a prospector I had seen years ago squatting beside a creek washing gravel in a gold pan. Once the gulch had swarmed with miners; now the hills were silent, purple in the autumn haze, and I could hear the trickle of water and the whisper of falling leaves.

The prospector wore bib-overalls, a hat with a sweat-stained band, and a beard roughened his jaw. Arthritis had swollen the knuckles of his hands.

"Have you had any luck?"

"I been panning about a buck a day."

A dollar a day was thirty dollars a month, enough to buy groceries and an occasional bottle of cheap whiskey. The cabin from which the prospector had cleared the pack rats cost no money—it was a relic of the gold rush. Such a life seemed harsh and solitary.

For a long while I watched the prospector shaking the gravel in his pan, pouring out water, adding a little more.

The old man had little chance to find gold in commercial quantities. More than half a century ago the creek and the surrounding ridges had been exhaustively sampled by hopeful miners. I thought of how a writer in the 1860s described a prospector as a man who lost all relish for society and thought of nothing but the success with which he was one day to meet in the pursuit of gold. Yet, when and if he made a discovery, often a better one was farther on, and the prospector would desert a good claim to look for another, in the end dying destitute and alone.

The opportunity to strike it rich is not possible today to the technicians at Santa Rita. The Chino Division of Kennecott Copper, which operates the open pit as well as the nearby smelter, claims there are 600 job classifications at Chino, but not one of the 1,450 employees is listed as a miner. The men who work the machines make more money and live better than the prospector could have imagined, and he—the individual—has been replaced by teams of scientists and skilled workers. Engineers, surveyors, and earth scientists are today's prospectors. They depend on helicopters for transportation and on the latest procedures for chemical and spectrographic analysis in mobile laboratories for testing the minerals.

Recently, millions of acres in the western Primitive areas were surveyed by geologists from the United States Bureau of Mines. This was done so that all minerals in the United States would be discovered and classified. We met two of the geologists in the Selway Wilderness Area of northern Idaho, where rattlesnakes breed on the dry hills that have been scarred by fires. The geologists were on foot and we were on horseback. Above the trail the mountain rose steeply; on the other side it dropped hundreds of feet to the river, which meant the horses could not leave the trail. The geologists could have scrambled up the hill, but they refused to do so. "Not on your life!" a bearded young fellow told us. "Do you think I'm going to go into those bushes where there might be snakes?" The geologists backtracked a quarter of a mile to a clearing where no rattlesnakes could possibly be concealed.

An old-time prospector would have snorted in disgust at such unabashed cowardice and would have .demanded to know how, if the geologists refused to leave the trail, they could locate minerals. However, the prospector would have underestimated the young scientists and modern technology that is more efficient than any man could be with a pick and shovel. The old-time methods were adequate when the streams were rich in placer gold, but they will not do now, when minerals are scarce and varied.

The truth is that the bearded fellow with the burro and the shovel has been glamorized by legends that originated in the days of the gold rush, when the first prospectors looked for placers—that is, gold in gulches or streams that was exposed and washed down by erosion and that could be found in the form of nuggets or flakes. Placers were the poor man's chance of a fortune. Anyone with luck could locate a placer and work it—or so it was believed. The shoveling, the sluicing, the drifting and cradling the gravel demanded hard physical labor, but it did not need technical skill or a large capital investment. All a man needed in the 1860s was a pick, a shovel, a gold pan, some bacon, flour, coffee, blankets, a bowie knife, and a revolver. Sometimes he had a saddle horse and pack mule.

When gold was discovered in California, emigration surged to that area, bypassing the Rocky Mountains where the arid land discouraged settlement. Only the Mormons, disciplined by Brigham Young, seemed unaffected by the fever. In Zion it was more desirable to plant a peach tree than to search for an elusive fortune in the hills. From 1850 to 1860 the population of the Pacific coast grew faster than that of the Rocky Mountain area. When the California placers became overcrowded and began to play out, when gold was discovered on the Gila River in Arizona, near Denver in 1859 and, shortly thereafter, at Oro Fino in Idaho—which was followed by a strike on Alder Gulch in what is now Montana—the tide reversed itself, and from 1860 to 1900 the population of the Rocky Mountain area grew faster than that of the Pacific Coast.

Mining camps sprang up, sometimes literally overnight. Where there had been wilderness, swarmed thousands of men. When the placers were exhausted and a new strike stampeded the miners to another gulch, the camp was deserted as quickly as it had materialized. No thought was given to brutalizing the land—the idea, get rich and get out. The gold rush created a frenetic, heedless, and unstable population.

One of these gold camps was described by Albert Richardson, an editorial writer for the *New York Tribune*, who visited Denver and the nearby Gregory diggings in the summer of 1859. Denver had become a supply point for the mines and was destined to grow into a city, but in 1859 it was a frontier town where the buildings were of log chinked with mud.

Richardson described it this way. He was traveling with his editor, Horace Greeley—the famous abolitionist who wore steel-rimmed glasses and chin whiskers and disapproved strongly of liquor and gambling.

"Denver," Richardson wrote, "contained about one thousand people, with three hundred buildings, nearly all of hewn pine logs. One-third were unfinished and roofless, having been erected the previous winter for speculative purposes. There were very few glass windows or doors and but two or three board floors. The nearest saw-mill was forty miles away, and the occupants of the cabins lived upon the native earth, hard, smooth and clean-swept. One lady, by sewing together corn-sacks for a carpet and covering her log walls with sheets and table cloths, gave to her mansion an appearance of rare luxury. Chairs were glories yet to come . . . . Chimneys were of sticks of wood piled up like children's cob-houses and plastered with mud. A few roofs were covered with shingles split by hand, but most were of logs spread with prairie grass and covered with earth. . . .

"Denver society was a strange medley. There were Americans from every quarter of the Union, Mexicans, Indians, half-breeds, trappers, speculators, gamblers, desperados, broken-down politicians and honest men. Almost every day was enlivened by its little shooting match. . . .

"We took lodgings at the Denver House. True to the national instinct, the occupants of its great drinking and gambling saloon demanded a speech. On one side the tipplers at the bar silently sipped their grog; on the other the gamblers respectfully suspended the shuffling of cards and the counting of money from their huge piles of coin, while Mr. Greeley standing between them, made a strong anti-drinking and anti-gambling address, which was received with perfect good humor."

The diggings were forty miles northwest of Denver in a narrow canyon jammed with log cabins, wagons, tents, oxen and men who were digging and shoveling dirt into sluice boxes. So frantic was the atmosphere that the miners refused to recognize the fact that only a few were panning enough gold to make the labor worthwhile.

"Little time is required to learn the great truth," Richardson wrote, "that digging gold is about the hardest way on earth to obtain it."

The population of the mining camps was young and mobile and, for the most part, optimistic. Men looked into the future, not the past. Many camps burst with civic pride, despite heaps of gravel in the gulches, mud in the streets, and the flimsy buildings. The suffix "City" was an example of the optimism that more often proved to be misleading than prophetic. The more stable inhabitants felt that their camp was going to be a prosperous community when the railroad arrived. Richardson wrote that when he asked a Colorado resident if his camp had a church, the gentleman replied, no, it did not but they expected to build one before the next Sunday.

Nathaniel Langford, who lived in Virginia City, Montana—the boomtown on Alder Gulch—believed that "The daring, adventurous and courageous elements of character are necessarily developed and brought into frequent action in a mining community." Such an environment developed ingenuity and confidence, but it also emphasized physical labor at the expense of intellectual attainments. Nor were miners more racially tolerant than other people on the frontier. Indians and Chinese were frequently subjected to gross injustice.

By 1877 the stampedes had receded to the Black Hills of the Dakotas, and the thrifty Chinese, who flocked in from the West Coast, mined the heaps of gravel left behind by the white men.

Mining entered a new phase; the time of the individual was past. Precious metals still existed in quartz lodes, but quartz lodes, to be exploited, demanded capital investment for heavy machinery and hired labor. Eastern financiers entered the picture, investing outright in western mines or issuing stock that started speculation in mining shares, which was to dominate the Rocky Mountain financial scene for many years.

Men who had formerly worked for themselves were forced to work for wages in the mines. Those who insisted on prospecting independently could not understand that the odds against them had increased. In quartz lodes the ore could turn out to be in pockets or the veins could disappear; while silver and copper were not valuable enough alone to mine unless the ore was produced in quantities. Still, men invested what money they had or could borrow in countless claims they were sure would become bonanzas.

In small prospect holes as well as the large mines, working conditions were worse than they had been in the placers. In the hot desert sun men hauled buckets of earth from shafts they had dug with pick and shovel. In underground tunnels miners swung sledge hammers, drilled, and blasted. The powder was tricky and the caps sometimes exploded. In Virginia City, Nevada, below the 3,000-foot level the heat rose to 138 degrees, and the miners worked in seven-minute shifts with the sweat pouring from their bodies.

In any mine a cave-in could crush a man beneath fallen timbers or doom him to death by suffocation. Fire could trap him underground, to be burned, or he could be drowned by water flooding the shafts.

"I remember," a miner from Butte, Montana, told me, "an old-timer saying that the ventilation was so poor in the mines that his head ached all the time."

The independent prospector knew that others had struck it rich, why couldn't he?

Ed Schliffin was a symbol. Schliffin—gaunt, six-foot, bearded—refused to be discouraged by years of prospecting and discovered the vein of silver in Arizona that made him a fortune and the town of Tombstone one of the best known of the later-day mining camps. Schliffin had faith and patience, men told themselves, and that's what it took. But Schliffin was also fortunate in that he had the support of a mining engineer and financial backing.

The refusal to be discouraged is evident today in Tombstone, whose old-time wooden buildings cling to the arid hills of southern Arizona. Tourism, not mining, produced the income in Tombstone, which is noted for the O.K. Corral and the Crystal Palace Bar—haunt of Wyatt Earp and Doc Holliday. But in 1968 the inhabitants were talking about the mines that had reopened since the price controls on silver had been lifted.

"You'll see mining around here again, mark my words," the bartender in the Crystal Palace told us.

The die-hards, who still believe the individual can strike it rich, point to Charles Augustus Steen. In the summer of 1952, with a $600 grubstake and a borrowed Geiger counter, he staked a claim on the Big Indian Wash near Moab, Utah. Steen was a bespectacled, thirty-one-year-old geologist, who lived with his wife in a tar-paper shack he rented for fifteen dollars a week. Skeptics called the geologist's claim "Steen's Folly," but they did not laugh when the claim turned out to be the largest uranium deposit in North America, and worth $60 million. In the tradition of many who had struck it rich in the old days, Steen spent his fortune with a lavish hand, building a million-dollar mansion in Reno, Nevada, and entertaining at a party for 8,000 guests; investing in cattle ranches and airlines. By 1969 Steen was bankrupt and had to borrow money to buy groceries, but, again, in the western tradition, he accepted full responsibility.

Time magazine quoted him as saying, "Money is made to be spent and I've spent it, . . . But for the most part, people with money bore the hell out of me."

Steen resembled mining magnates such as Horace Tabor, who made his fortune in silver, married Baby Doe, and squandered his dollars on such luxuries as a hotel carpeted in red plush and ornamented with a sixty-foot bar and one-ton crystal chandeliers. Other mining magnates, shrewder than Tabor or Steen, kept their fortunes. These were men such as John MacKay, Jim Fair, and William Sharon, who were called the Bonanza Kings because their money came from the Comstock Lode. Then, there was Tom Walsh who, like Tabor, struck it rich in Colorado. Walsh's Camp Bird Mine at Ouray proved so valuable that his daughter was able to buy the Hope Diamond. In Montana William A. Clark made millions in copper from the Richest Hill on Earth at Butte. These men spent little of their money in the states that produced it. Their ambitions included twenty-room mansions, financial expansion into other fields, ambassadorships, and election to the United States Senate. Socially ambitious wives preferred to forget their humble beginnings in San Francisco or New York. W. A. Clark, for instance, endowed the Los Angeles Symphony and an art museum in Washington, D. C., but he did not give a cent to Montana where he had made his fortune, nor did MacKay or Flood feel responsibility to Nevada.

When the Comstock Lode was paying off, Virginia City, Nevada, was the queen of the mining camps. Big money meant big spending in those expansionist days of the frontier. A half-million-dollar Opera House boasted gilded pillars and scarlet plush drapes. Saloons lined their walls with expensive mirrors and larger-than-life oil paintings in carved gilt frames.

The lawlessness as well as the boisterous extravagance of the "Gilded Age" generated legends whose appeal is as bold today as it was generations ago. Men can hope for the luck of Charles Augustus Steen and can chuckle at the extravagant indiscretions of the mining magnates. This is part of the western myth.

Glossed over and forgotten were the men whose hopes did not materialize, who in those boom times labored to produce the wealth for the fortunate few. These were the hard-rock miners whose life and whose families' lives were described by Annie Ellis in a book called *The Story of an*

Ordinary Woman.

Annie grew up in an atmosphere of violence. The mines shut down frequently and without warning, and, when they did, it meant hunger in the camps because there was no relief, no pension plan or compensation—although labor was beginning to fight for reforms. In 1893 in Butte, Montana, the Western Federation of Miners was organized. The Union activities reached far into the Rocky Mountain states, but Annie had little sympathy with strikes because strikes meant no wages. At the time miners received three dollars a day for an eight-hour shift.

Annie's mother did laundry, carrying water in buckets from the creek so that she could earn enough to buy milk to feed her children. When she had a baby, she bore it alone because a miner's wages did not permit a doctor. Annie's underwear was made of flour sacks, and the family lived in a cabin that had a ceiling covered with canvas where the rats nested. Once Annie's mother stuck a pitchfork into a rat and the blood dripped through the canvas; the little girl cried, not because of the blood—she'd seen men crushed in the mines— but because of the indignity of such a life. Annie never had a chance. She loved books and reading, but school was an unobtainable luxury to a miner's child. While still young, Annie married a miner and followed him to the boomtowns until he was killed in an explosion.

In Goldfield, Nevada, Annie's child died, and, having no money to buy a gravestone, she stole a granite step from a schoolhouse and dragged it to the cemetery.

No, people did not want to hear stories like that. They did not want to acknowledge that competitive enterprise had been supplanted by monopoly and that, in time, the mining magnates—lucky, unscrupulous, tough, call them what you will—would be supplanted by corporations.

Above all, they did not want to relinquish the western myth.

Goldfield, Nevada, prospered long after the Comstock Lode ceased producing but, by then, the bonanza period of mining had come to an end. The richest and most available ore had been exploited. Production costs had increased, and the price of gold and silver had declined. A final blow was the repeal of the Sherman Silver Purchase Act in 1893, from which the mines never recovered.

Today the metals that are proving feasible to produce are copper, zinc, aluminum, molybdenum and nickel—all metals that received a boost from space exploration. The vast reserves of coal in southeastern Montana, in Wyoming and Colorado are creating new interest with the announcement of a number of coal-burning power plants to be built in the future. Added incentives to coal mining are new methods that reduce costs. Technology was also aided in the production of gas and oil by means of nuclear blasts. In Colorado in the fall of 1969, a forty-kiloton explosion was detonated at a depth of 8,430 feet. Nuclear explosions, according to the Project Coordinator for Basic Production Research for the United States Bureau of Mines, can make available trillions of cubic feet of gas. Oil can also be extracted by new methods, which is important in regard to the extensive oil shale rock deposits in western Colorado, southern Wyoming, and eastern Utah that are estimated to contain $300 billion worth of oil and trillions of cubic feet of natural gas. Until the application of atomic energy to deeply buried reserves, they were unavailable for exploitation.

The development of natural resources on such a scale demands not only the capital of the large oil companies, but the participation of the government as well. In these operations there is little room for the independent individual.

Today the old mining shafts are choked with rock and rotting timbers, and if you inquire about investing in mining, this is what you will be told: "Don't put your money in a gold mine, put it in a gravel pit."

The Rancher -- Cattle, Oil, and Quarter Horses

IV

If you drive through the Rocky Mountain West, you will see cattle in every state from the high, windy plateaus of eastern Montana and Wyoming to the Sonora Desert in Arizona. The cattle are Black Angus, Hereford, creamy Charlois, and short-horns; many of the Hereford and Angus calves are mixed, for ranchers have discovered advantages in cross-breeding. The bulls are big and well muscled and have prize blood lines. Seldom do you see the scrub cattle that predominated before World War II. In the autumn when the cattle have been brought down from the summer range, they graze on the fields where the hay has been cut and stacked. The stubbled fields are the color of honey, and the mountains, white with snow, cut into the blue sky. The barns and the ranch houses are newly painted, and there is a television antenna on the roof of the house and a new pick-up truck in the yard. What a life, you think enviously, and wish you might live so well in such surroundings. Ranching, you think, must be a prosperous business. This is a mistake. Ranching, except for brief periods, has never been an industry that produced a sizable income for many people.

Like mining, ranching has experienced changes in the Rocky Mountain West, although the changes have not been as drastic or as widespread. Ranchers still pride themselves because—unlike wheat farmers and the airlines—they are not subsidized by the government, at least not directly. They like to think of themselves as the last of a vanishing breed that was typified by the old-time cowman—bluff, honest, hardworking, and, above all, independent.

The question is, who are the ranchers fooling—themselves or the public? One of the most enduring myths of the West is the cowboy, and the suspicion exists that the rancher finds himself in the interesting position of being a nineteenth-century myth that has carried over into the twentieth.

A growing belief is that the rancher is an anachronism and that he should be phased out. Mention this to a rancher and he explodes. To destroy the western cattle rancher would be to strike a fatal blow to free enterprise, which was responsible for the growth of the United States into a great nation.

Undeniable, however, is the fact that the rancher is in trouble and that he resents the public's charges that he is responsible for the high price of beef.

Walter Burris of the Andrada Ranch south of Tucson, Arizona, told me that he felt the rancher has a bad image.

What Burris meant was that the popular impression of a cattleman is a man in a big hat and high-heeled boots driving a Cadillac, whose wealth is in cattle, oil, and quarter horses. This impression, Burris felt, was due to the Texans.

Burris himself looked like the image he deplored, although I do not remember his driving a Cadillac. He was a big man; his jeans belted beneath a paunch, leather-skinned, with small, shrewd, grey eyes. Reticent about his personal affairs, he was willing enough to talk about cattle. In this respect he was typical of ranchers in other parts of the Rocky Mountain area.

His Andrada Ranch comprised 100,000 acres of desert, broken by dry sandy arroyos withering in the sun. Most of the ranch was government leased. Burris said it was the finest stock country in the West. When I asked what the cattle ate, he waved his hand at the mesquite and prickly pear. "Everything you see growing." Protein and carbohydrates were provided by cake fed on the range. The size of the ranch and of others in the Southwest became understandable when Burris said he figured sixty acres per cow.

To all appearances the one-story ranch house with a swimming pool typified security and a good life, but Burris contradicted this: "The high price of land and labor are driving us out of business. You have to pay a foreman $500 a month, a hand $250 to $300. My help are all Mexicans; you don't have to pay them so much."

"If the ranchers aren't making a profit," I said, "then, who is?"

"The middleman," Burris said, "and the supermarkets. The supermarkets control prices."

Burris's opinion of the supermarkets was not shared by the majority of ranchers.

"What about government subsidies?"

Burris reacted with the expected vehemence. "We don't want government help! We don't want government people telling us what to do; they're inexperienced in the cattle business."

"What's going to happen, then?"

"I don't know, but the ranchers should organize. All users of the public lands should organize, like the miners."

Burris was silent for a minute, guiding the pickup along a hot, dry ridge. The road was no more than a track in the sand that avoided the saguaro cactus and mesquite. Burris was a capable driver; he should have been, he spent as much of his time in a pickup as he did on a horse.

"The most help I get," Burris said, "is from the University Agriculture Department. They tell the ranchers about new feeds, new methods."

In 1967 it was estimated that the Arizona rancher made a profit of only $1.92 average per cow unit. The small margin of profit and the hard work—for the rancher does work hard, despite mechanization—offer little incentive to young people to go into the business. Nor is there the glamor that once was attached to ranching. The cowboy has been supplanted by the astronaut, the motorcycle racer, the scientist, and the politician.

Jasper Ackerman, rancher and banker of Colorado Springs, told us, as we toured the rococo magnificence of the Broadmore Hotel, that a young man could not afford to go into ranching if he had to buy land and cattle and make a living from it, unless he had $100 thousand to invest.

"The price of land has gone up to such an extent," Ackerman said, "that the rancher can't afford to buy it, and this is at a time that government leases are being cut down."

Jim Edwards, who has a cow-calf operation in the Ruby Valley in southwestern Montana, enumerated other problems facing the rancher: beef imports, grazing fee increases on public lands, taxes, the listing of cattle, like the listing of grain, on the future's market, which—so Edwards thought—lessened the rancher's say on the price of his product; the increase in the cost of labor, machinery, feed, and medicines.

Concerning the cost squeeze, all ranchers agree. They also agree that the middleman and not the rancher is getting the largest share of the profits and is responsible for the high price of beef to the consumer.

"Twenty years ago," Tom Barbour—a rancher from Ovando, Montana—declared, "a rancher could make a living with one hundred cows. Now, he has to have twice that many."

In the northern Rocky Mountain states, where Mexican help is not available, the rancher is fortunate if he has a family to help with the work. Many times, ranch wives struggle through the snow in below-zero weather to rescue a calf.

In Salmon, Idaho, we talked to a tall, skinny fellow with greying hair at his temples. We had bought some horses from him the previous year, and, when he saw us eating lunch at the café where he had just finished a meal, he stopped to greet us. I asked how he was getting along, and he shrugged ruefully.

"Working hard. I got a job on the highway. It takes two jobs to keep going, nowdays."

"Who takes care of the ranch?"

"My wife. She's pretty handy, but she don't get as much time as she'd like to break out colts anymore."

All over the West ranch women are driving tractors and stock trucks, irrigating, haying, vaccinating, dehorning, and helping with the calving.

Ken Kautz, manager of the Bitterroot Stock Farm—one of the most up-to-date ranches in Montana with regard to its breeding program and range management—said, "The small, independent operator is being driven out of business.

His profit margin is so small that he can't afford a poor calf crop, or a drop of a few cents in price, or a new piece of equipment, or getting hurt and being laid up."

Figures confirm Kautz's statement. In Wyoming the ranches in the late 1960s were more than double the size they were in 1935; the average was 3,600 acres in 1969. In Montana over the last thirty years, the total farm population, as in all the western states, has steadily grown smaller until only 15.6 percent of the total population in Montana—which in 1969 listed agriculture as a chief source of income—was engaged in farming. At the same time the ranches have grown larger. In Nevada the average size of a ranch in the late 1960s was 2,880 acres and in Colorado in 1969 it was 1,161 acres, whereas in Colorado in 1910 it was 293 acres.

What the figures do not tell is that some ranches have been cut up into what real estate people call "parcels" and have ceased to exist as agricultural units.

The surprising part is not that the little, independent rancher is facing extinction but that ranchers have continued to operate for as long as they have. The fur traders and the placer miners are gone; only the ranchers, relics of the Old West, remain, and they are fighting the same fundamental problems that they did in the nineteenth century—weather, dependence on the public domain, and distance from markets. So far, even in this age of technology, the weather is beyond human control. As for public domain, the rancher depends, in the majority of cases, on land that he does not own to graze his stock. This is done under the Taylor Grazing Act of 1934 that permits so many head of stock to graze on public domain for a fixed fee. Additional acres of national forest were also opened for this purpose under the Multiple-Use-Sustained Yield Act of 1960.

In the West an astonishing amount of land is owned by

the federal government and a lesser but still sizable amount is owned by the states. In Wyoming the federal government alone lists 30 percent of the state's land area as public domain; that is, land left in federal ownership because the homesteaders found it too arid, mountainous, or far from water to settle. Another 20 percent of the land is included in national parks and forests. This is a total of 50 percent of the land in Wyoming and does not include state and local government-owned lands or Indian reservations. Of Montana's 147,138 square miles, 30 percent is administered by the federal government; in Utah two-thirds of the state's area is in a similar category; in Nevada 86 percent of the land is federally owned; in Idaho more than two-thirds is federally owned; in New Mexico—which has a total of 77.8 million acres—27 million acres belong to the federal government, 11.5 million to the state, and 6.3 million are Indian lands. Colorado ranks lowest in the amount of land owned by the federal government—36 percent.

Most of the land that is not in a national forest, park, monument, or Indian reservation is only suited for grazing. Much of this land is in places where only sheep and goats can survive, and there are millions of acres where not even those hardy beasts can live, areas that are as desolate and bleak as the surface of the moon. All the land that could be farmed was taken up by the homesteaders, but not even the Mormons could grow crops on alkali or basalt, where the rainfall averaged less than twelve inches annually and where there was no water within a hundred miles.

The federal lands that concern the rancher most are administered by the Forest Service, the Bureau of Land Management, and the Bureau of Reclamation. One of the difficulties that affect the rancher today is the increasing pressure of a growing population on these public lands, particularly for recreation.

The distances from markets remains what it was in the 1880s with slight variations, such as the growth of markets on the West Coast and, to some extent, the metropolitan centers of Denver, Phoenix, and Salt Lake City. Cattle also go to Omaha and Iowa rather than to the big, old-time packing plants in Chicago and Kansas City, but it is still a long way from the Montana ranges to the feeders in the Midwest.

In the fall of 1969 we watched a trainload of cattle bound for Omaha pull out of the Bitterroot Valley in western Montana. The scene could have been repeated in countless places in the West. The cattle were owned by a number of ranchers, and half a dozen went along to care for the stock and to water them on the one stop scheduled on the trip. They traveled in what was called a drover's car that had a stove for warmth and bunks where the men could spread their bedrolls. Owen Wister's Virginian would have been right at home, except the ranchers were middle-aged, their once broad shoulders stooped from hard labor and their stomachs thickening above still lean hips.

In Omaha the cattle would be sold to farmers who would fatten them on grain and sell them to the packers. The corn and sorghums that these farmers raised were guaranteed by federal subsidies, which made farming a profitable business in the Midwest.

The rancher is a different breed from the midwestern farmer, and the difference goes back to the days when ranching began to boom with the railroad that made it possible to ship beef from western ranges to midwestern packing plants. Land was available to anyone, and in many instances cattlemen did not bother to make formal declarations of ownership; there seemed no need when in the northern states much of the land was unsurveyed, and in the Southwest much of the land was claimed by Spanish grants that were easily abrogated. This assumption of ownership of a large amount of the range created an arrogance in the cattlemen that was not typical of the miners or fur traders. The blame for appropriating land could not be entirely put upon the ranchers; the government encouraged settlement and the method of doing it invited fraud. In 1862 the Homestead Law had been enacted, by which a man might acquire 160 acres. In 1873 the Timber Culture Act was passed, and in 1877 the Desert Land Act. Already enacted was the Preemption Act of 1841 that entitled a man to squat on land, surveyed or unsurveyed, until it was put up for sale. The act also entitled the man to have the first chance to buy up to 160 acres at $1.25 an acre.

The fact that these small acreages were sufficient for a family in the humid, forested areas of the East but far from adequate in the arid regions of the West, where distance to water in most areas was measured in miles, did not occur to Congress. If a rancher wanted to raise cattle, he had to acquire additional land by unlawfully fencing the public domain, or by requiring his cowboys to take up all the land they could under the Land Acts and then deed it to him, or, by stratagem, obtain title to Spanish grants. Eventually, over 80 percent of the Spanish-Mexican grants went to American lawyers or settlers.

The historian Ernest Staples Osgood wrote that the basis of the cattle business was "free pasture of those unoccupied and unused leagues of the public domain open to all."

In regard to water, the laws for its usage were passed by legislatures dominated by mining. The eight Rocky Mountain states developed the Arid Region Doctrine of prior appropriation, which meant that the first person to file on the water had first water rights to use or to divert a certain number of inches of water for his own purposes on a stream or river. This abrogation of the English Common Law of riparian rights, which was, and still is, followed in the East and to a modified extent in the rest of the country, came about because of the use of water in placer operations in the days of the gold rush.

In 1878 John Wesley Powell in his report, *Lands of the Arid Region of the United States*, recommended classification of lands into mineral, timber, coal, irrigable, and pasturage areas. The survey system, Powell felt, should be changed and the Homestead Act modified to fit the West. Powell recognized, if Congress did not, that vast areas of the West were suited only for grazing and also that water should be designated as an all-important topographical feature. The ranchers, Powell felt, should have 2,560 acres with access to water. In other words, the rancher and the farmer, who were the two groups that would utilize the land, should not be regarded as having the same needs.

The reaction of the ranchers to this was that they were doing all right as they were and that any change might bring speculators and eastern land sharks to monopolize the range.

At the time, the ranchers were well situated. The range in the northern Rocky Mountain area was not crowded, particularly in Wyoming and Montana. Colorado had more cattle than the range could support without overgrazing, but the ranchers were not unduly concerned. In Colorado cattle had first begun as a business along the Arkansas River and its tributaries, and west over the Sangre de Cristos Mountains. In New Mexico cattle grazed on the old Spanish land grants, and in Nevada cattle grazed the length of the Humboldt Valley, where emigrants bound for the Sierra gold fields had been trailing sheep, cows, and horses since 1849. But until the end of the Civil War and the construction of the railroad, the cattle market had been local. The Union Pacific, the Sante Fe, and the Northern Pacific opened up eastern markets so that ranching became big business. An added boost was the development of the tin can and artificial refrigeration that enabled the midwestern meat packers to dominate the market by buying cheap western cattle to sell as beef in population centers that had previously depended on local sources.

So the trail herds started north, bawling in the dust, to shipping points in Abilene and Ogallala; to stock the plains of Colorado, Wyoming and Montana.

In other states and territories mining rivaled ranching; in Wyoming ranching had no rival. At the same time what happened in that territory happened to a certain extent in all the Rocky Mountain regions, which is the reason Wyoming customarily serves as a study for the cattle industry.

At the same time that the trail herds were coming up from Texas, over the mountains to the west came herds descended from the Durhams brought to Oregon by the emigrants. These, as well as the Longhorns, were to stock the endless miles of grassland, which were now open to the rancher. The buffalo had been slaughtered and the Indians, who had once proved a barrier to settlement, had been penned on reservations, partly due to complaints from the cattlemen who saw no reason why the Indians should monopolize an area suited to grazing.

Driving the trail herds were lean, sunbaked men who, within a short span of time, were to personify the romance of the West. These were the cowboys, master horsemen, experts with a rope and a gun, young and reckless and clad in a costume, derived from the Mexicans, of chaps and broad-brimmed hat. The cowboy's job was perilous, and the backdrop against which he played his role was the vast, cloud-shadowed deserts of the West.

Few writers told of the lack of security in a cowboy's life, the low wages that did not permit a family, the lack of education, the drabness of the cowtowns where the cowboy had to find recreation in saloons with false fronts and odorous privies. Socially a cowboy was no more than a hired hand.

The more ambitious cowboys became ranchers, and in the 1860s and 1870s this was not difficult. A contemporary of this time wrote that most ranchers possessed "great personal strength and endurance." The independent cattlemen had to be strong in those days. They fought the railroads, the Indians, sheepmen, homesteaders, each other and, always, the land. In the end it was the land that brought an end to the bonanza days of the open range. But in the boom decades before 1886-87, the cattlemen created a legend as high, wide, and handsome as the West itself.

Until the 1870s the Wyoming rancher was a frontier figure with his only investment in his cattle that he grazed on the public domain. By the late seventies the range became crowded with cattle, and the big outfits financed by eastern and foreign capital had begun to dominate the scene. This expansion was partly due to speculators and developers, and partly to publicists hired by the railroads. The more settlers who moved West, the more freight the railroads would carry, and cattle proved unexpectedly profitable as a commodity to the western lines.

Typical of those who extolled the West was James Brisbin, who wrote: "The West! The mighty West . . . where the broad rivers flow and the boundless prairie stretches away for thousands of miles; where new states are every year carved out and myriads of people find homes and wealth; where the poor, professional young man, flying from the overcrowded East and the tyranny of a moneyed aristocracy, finds honor and wealth . . . where there are lands for the landless." Profits in the cattle business, Brisbin insisted, could run as high as 25 percent.

If they could not become ranchers themselves, people invested in land and cattle companies. Promoters formed syndicates, bought cattle, and grazed them on the public domain under the care of a resident manager and foreman. So great was the demand for cattle to stock these new northern ranges that the buyers had trouble filling their orders.

Big money created big outfits whose brands became known from the Sierras to the Missouri. The Swan Land and Cattle Company, which was sold to a Scottish syndicate, ran 160,000 head of cattle. In southwestern Wyoming three outfits controlled 75 percent of the range in an empire that extended from the Utah border on the west to the Continental Divide east of Steamboat Springs, a distance of 150 miles. In northern Wyoming the Powder River Company, financed largely by Englishmen, ran 60,000 head.

Stock Growers Associations, to which these outfits belonged, wielded great political power, and some of their members were elected governor and senator, although ostensibly the associations were organized to regulate roundups, identify brands, define range boundaries, improve the breed of cattle, and fight disease.

In the capital of Wyoming Territory, the Cheyenne Club became one of the most famous private clubs in the West, where young Englishmen who would someday succeed to a title, wealthy sons of eastern families, writers, politicians, and army officers strolled the verandah smoking cheroots. In the evening six-course dinners with imported wines and oysters were served by white-jacketed waiters.

During this period the term "remittance man" became popular to describe the black sheep of a prominent family who was sent west to reform or, if that was impossible, at least to get him out of the way.

Ranching as a career or a hobby was considered socially

acceptable, and this is true today. A roster of ranchers in the Rocky Mountain West would list some of the most famous families in America and England. The autumn of 1969 saw Prince Philip, consort of Queen Elizabeth, visiting friends on a ranch in Sheridan, Wyoming.

The influx of educated easterners and titled Englishmen in the 1870s and 1880s aroused antagonism. The small ranchers and those who had worked hard to build their outfits into successful spreads did not like to see the range appropriated by absentee owners or by men who had so much hired help they did not have to do a thing themselves. In the West a man, no matter who he was, worked at his business whether it was mining or ranching, and he resented people like the Frewen brothers of the Powder River Cattle Company who kept relays of horses to gallop their guests from the railroad to palatial log ranch houses. Hothouse flowers from Denver were brought to the Powder River by the same means, and probably a welcome ornament they were in that arid country, but roses out of season in Wyoming did not agree with the westerner's idea of life on a cattle ranch, nor did racing across the prairie shouting "tally-ho" after coyotes.

In addition, the big foreign- and eastern-financed companies monopolized the range. A man could have 200 or 300 head of cattle grazing on the public domain with grass and access to water. One day an outfit invaded the range with eight thousand head, sweeping the small herd into the larger. If the rancher objected, the foreman told him to cut out his god-damned cows, but one man could not find a couple hundred head among eight thousand. What was more, the large herd grazed off the range, and the outfit of a dozen or more cowboys armed with pistols informed the rancher that the water was no longer his—they'd taken it over.

The absentee owner or the stockholders might not be

aware of the foreman's high-handed ways; all they were interested in was a return on their investment. When they visited the ranch, they saw the glamorous aspect of the business,
as they galloped across the prairie where the cattle grazed by
the thousands on hills the color of tarnished brass. The air was
scented with sage and dust and cattle dung. A cowboy shout-
ed, a cow bellowed for her calf. At night the campfires
sparked in a world of stars and shadows. In such an environment a man was free of the laws and traditions that bound
him in more settled areas.

When the small rancher was driven off the range, he had
no recourse to the law, for the law was a long way off in those
days and was often influenced by the Cattlemen's Association. To the cattleman the small, would-be rancher was a
squatter, but this was not always true; for the little man acquired his land by filing on a homestead. His threat to the
cattleman was that he, too, claimed part of the public domain
and, when he had it, he fenced it off with barbed wire. At the
same time other claimants to free land were appearing, mainly the sheepmen. But for the disasters that overtook the big
cattleman, his own greed was responsible. Cattle were shoved
onto the range until it became overgrazed. Continued high
prices for beef and an unusually long spell of good weather
led to overconfidence.

In November of 1886 the sky darkened and the wind
rose, a cold whisper increasing to a shriek across the high plateaus of Montana and Wyoming. The cattle, heads down,
backs humped, drifted with the blizzard. This was the first of
the storms that alternated with chinooks. A "killing winter,"
the Indians called it, and, as proof, told of the great, grey Arc-
tic owls that only appeared in times of severe cold. Steers
froze standing up or piled against barbed wire. Others were
buried by drifts. At night the wolves closed in to tear hunks of

flesh from still living animals. The Longhorns and the Durhams and the Herefords starved and then they froze with
their eyes iced shut and there was nothing the ranchers could
do. They had no hay and no shelter, and even if the cattle had
not been too weak to drive, no man or horse could have survived in the screaming, grey void of the storm.

When, at last, spring melted the snow and the freshets
began to flow across the prairie, the air stank of dead cattle.
The big outfits suffered the greatest loss. The Powder River
Cattle Company was bankrupt, and the Swan Land and Cattle Company went into receivership.

So passed "those lords of creation, the cattle kings."

After that bitter winter ranching was never the same.
Perhaps it would not have been, anyhow; the blizzards only
hastened the end of an era. From that time on the rancher
saw that if he would survive, he would have to practice range
management, have smaller and better-bred herds, cut hay for
winter fodder, and provide shelter. The realization did not
come easily or quickly. Ranchers did not like change; they
resent it today, and they resent the fact that physical stamina,
courage, and determination are not in themselves enough.
The ranchers continued to fight the homesteaders until all the
land that could be plowed—and some that couldn't—was
filed on. The ranchers are still fighting for a share of the
public domain; only this time they are fighting the government for an easing of grazing restrictions and a lowering of
the grazing fee through their congressmen, state legislatures,
and stockmen's associations.

They are also lobbying against beef imports.

Some experts feel that feed lots in the Rocky Mountain
area rather than in the Midwest are the solution, and there
are a number of such feeding operations in the region. Ken
Kautz, of the Bitterroot Stock Farm, suggested, half jokingly,

a roadside meat stand to sell directly to the public, and thus eliminate the middleman.

In the late 1960s and the early 1970s beef production was at an all time high. Efficient methods of feeding, breeding, and range management boosted the number of cattle shipped to the feed lots to figures that numbered in the hundreds of thousands. The rancher, understandably, felt that he was getting the short end of the deal when, despite the rising price of beef in the supermarkets, his profits did not rise too. He is the one who assumes risks; for calves can still get the scours and northers can still roar down from Canada and steers can still freeze to death against barbed wire fences, although hay, now, can be dropped by helicopter to cattle marooned in drifts.

Seldom does the rancher speak about his discouragement when his sons leave home. Like Walter Burris, ranchers are not talkative about personal matters, but ranchers have always been family men and traditionalists and hoped and expected that their sons would carry on and, in the past, this was the case. Today a rancher's obituary lists his survivors in California or Washington or perhaps Chicago. Every year ranches are sold by widows or by couples who are too old to work any longer, and many of the ranches are purchased by corporations. This is another thing the ranchers are worried about—the disappearance of the family unit in the take-over by corporations. Ranchers are afraid that ranching will become big business controlled by absentee owners who will deal with corporate processors and the huge wholesalers without regard to local people or local conditions. This is a very real concern, and signs of this happening can be seen throughout the West.

The family ranch might, indeed, become a relic of the past. In Arizona a study in 1969 showed that the average age of the rancher was fifty-seven. He was hanging onto his ranch and working it, but when he died or retired his land would be put on the market. If it was in an isolated area (such as eastern Montana or Wyoming), the chances were that it would be sold to a corporation; if it was near an urban area, it would be subdivided.

"When the ranchers are having such a hard time," I said to Ken Kautz, "why do they keep on ranching?"

"I dunno," he said, "It could be that it's a way of life, a good life, and they want to preserve it."

The Granger--The Plow
and Barbed Wire

V

On one of our horse trips to Arizona, we were accompanied by the same Mormon driver who had been with us in New Mexico. Our route followed Highway 93 south of Salt Lake, and in the spring dawn we could see apple blossoms washing like white foam against the base of the Wasatch Mountains. The trees in the orchards stood in symmetrical rows and the ground beneath them was carefully cultivated. At intervals we passed fields of lettuce, radish, and other vegetables, looking like gardens in a seed catalogue.

"How come," I said, "Mormon farms look better than other farms?"

Our Mormon friend smiled. "I suppose it's because

we're taught to be proud of being farmers."

The Mormons are in a minority in a part of the country where the bitterness of the homestead boom and bust is still remembered.

Farming does not mean the same thing in the West as it means in the East, where gentlemen farmers are identified with English country squires. In the West farming lacks status, and a man prefers to be a rancher, which is a traditionally respected profession.

Also, westerners go to some trouble to explain that states that are classified as agricultural, such as Montana, Idaho, and Wyoming, list timber and livestock as agricultural products which boosts the figures for agricultural production.

Montana, however, was the third largest producer of wheat in the nation in 1968, and the wheat farmer was one of the few persons engaged in raising crops other than forage, which predominates in the West. Unlike the cattleman, the wheat farmer has made money because he has been subsidized by the government. To the cattleman, battling for his independence, the wheat farmer is accepting thirty pieces of silver when he takes subsidies, but the farmer retorts that the cattleman has subsidies, too, only they are indirect.

In a public opinion poll, the people would side with the rancher in his big hat and cowboy boots.

The farmer, like the homesteader, has never become a mythical figure—overalls and a shovel are difficult to glamorize, and the farmer spends more time, today, riding a tractor than a horse. Indeed, he seldom has a horse or a cow on his place.

A typical wheat farmer was a friend in eastern Montana, who resembled an outdoor businessman—practical, college-educated, alert to the latest technological developments. He was franker than most wheat farmers would have been, and for that reason he did not want to be identified.

Wheat, he explained, like so many other things in the West, only became profitable after World War II when production shifted from the Southeast to the plains and the West. This shift was possible because of new fertilizers, drought-resistant strains of wheat, the invention of large machinery, and new methods of plowing and soil conservation. An added incentive—and a big one—was federal price-support programs, payment for nonproduction, and cost-share payments for conservation improvements to land. By these federal programs the government hoped to aid the little man and to halt a trend toward large, industrialized farms.

Our friend owned nearly three thousand acres. As I glanced at the white frame house with the TV aerial on the roof, the Piper Cub in a hangar, and the trees—the only ones within miles—shading the garden, I asked, "Have the federal programs succeeded?"

"They aren't a help to the little man today," our friend said. "I was lucky, I started out at the right time, so I could cash in on the subsidies. A young fellow trying to start out now couldn't make it. He'd have to have too big a capital to start with. In my case, with what I make on the farm, I pay my taxes and my living expenses and buy what machinery I need. I'm fully automated, you understand; I pay no wages, except, maybe, I hire a man during the harvest season. With my federal payment I buy more land to raise more wheat so I can get a larger wheat-program payment and buy more land."

If you drive through eastern Montana or parts of Wyoming or Idaho or Colorado, you will see the undulating hills, green in the spring with new wheat. In the autumn the straw-colored stubble unrolls for endless miles. The cultivation creates a geometric monotony of the land that is pleasing to those who like to be orderly. Occasionally you might see a shack like a dessicated shell on a treeless hill, and you will know that the surrounding 160 or 320 acres were filed on during the homestead boom by some emigrant who hoped to make a living in the West, and that when he sold out or, defeated, just left, so that his place "went for taxes," the subsidized wheat farmer—like our friend—added the homestead to his thousands of acres.

No myth created greater heartbreak than that of the agrarian utopia that led to the homesteaders—predecessors of the wheat farmer.

Today few homesteaders or their descendants remain on the land they settled in the late 1890s and the first two decades of this century. The depression of the thirties broke the last of them. When we moved to our ranch in western Montana in 1932, our closest neighbors were homesteaders, and not for many years did I realize they represented the lost dream of the agrarian utopians. However, our neighbors were fortunate because they had located in western Montana where the winters might be cold, but at least there were water and trees. Otherwise, the neighbors struggled to make a living, as did all homesteaders, by raising a few cows, planting a few crops, and being as self-sufficient as possible. They had their own chickens, pigs, and vegetable garden. Their sole income was derived from selling a cow now and then and cream to the local creamery.

We had no cow, so every other day my brothers or I rode horseback to the neighbors to bring back a pail of milk. Part of the way the trail followed the riverbank overgrown with cottonwoods. In the autumn the frost touched the trees so that the horse's hoofs thudded on golden leaves. Golden leaves floated on the water, spiraled downward in the still air, and above my head and all around was the shimmer and the glow of gold.

Enchanted, I exclaimed to our neighbor when I reached my destination, "Aren't the cottonwoods beautiful?"

Florence poured milk from a galvanized bucket into my pail. In the gloom of the barn, bony-hipped cows chewed their cud or raised their tails to splash manure. The floor was slimed with dung, and one end of the barn roof had collapsed and was propped with a pole.

In the corral chickens bickered among the rusted remains of a mower and tangles of barbed wire. The milk that we didn't buy would slop the pigs or go to the separator on the porch of the log house where Florence lived with her tubercular brother and eighty-year-old mother. The mother, who resembled a scarecrow, was hoeing the withered remnants of her garden while the brother was cutting wood, his racking cough echoing with the blows of his ax. Florence's greying hair was bobbed, and she wore overalls and a man's workshirt.

"What cottonwoods?"

I explained. "The cottonwoods by the river."

"I never noticed them." Florence picked up the bucket. "I don't have time to notice much."

Youth is intolerant, and when I reached home, I snorted to my mother. "You'd think that Florence would, at least, look at those cottonwoods!"

"When you work as hard as Florence," Mother said, "you are too tired to look at anything."

Mother's fingers rested on her knitting needles, and she sighed.

"Poor Florence, they say she used to be quite pretty when she first came to the valley."

"Well, she isn't pretty now! And she smells! The whole place smells!"

The sour smell of poverty and despair. I didn't recognize it then, although, instinctively, it revolted and frightened me.

That is the way it was with countless homesteaders. On the high plains east of the mountains and in Colorado, Idaho, and Wyoming, the situation was worse. The arid regions of Arizona, Nevada, and New Mexico had failed to attract farmers. Only Utah, because of the Mormons, occupied a unique position.

Murals in state capitols depicting women in sunbonnets with curly-haired children clinging to their skirts and bronzed men tilling fields of grain are an illusion of the agrarian utopia.

In the nineteenth century and the first decades of the twentieth, labor joined forces with the intellectuals to promote free land, but their efforts might have proved ineffective if the industrialists and financiers had not begun to see profit in the public domain. During this period the East Coast was deluged by a flood of emigration from Germany and Ireland. Factory owners no longer had to fear a labor shortage if workers moved from the cities to farms. At the same time businessmen saw an added advantage to developing the West: a rapidly expanding economy demanded new markets, and western farms could provide those markets.

To encourage settlement the Homestead Law was revised to permit the entry of 320 acres instead of 160, and in 1912 the residence requirements were shortened. Congress, also, belatedly recognized that the government must finance irrigation projects to water the arid acres plowed by the homesteaders, for the farmers themselves could not construct large irrigation projects, and private companies (as they did in the panic of 1893) often went bankrupt. Water, scarce enough in the West, was made even scarcer when cattlemen filed every water right they possibly could, while promoters seized springs and "rented" water at exorbitant rates. Nor were the homesteaders without fault. If possible, they filed on foothill land where small streams could be diverted to irrigation. If the streams had been allowed to flow unimpeded, the water could have irrigated more acres of better land at lower levels. Like everyone else, the homesteader was motivated, not for the general good or for the land, but for himself.

In 1894 Congress passed the Carey Act, whose purpose was to encourage the investment of capital in irrigation projects, but, due to various lopeholes, it succeeded mainly in giving corporations and speculators control of public lands. This was evident in Colorado. A more practical piece of legislation was the Newlands Act of 1902 that made provision for the Reclamation Service. Receipts from land sales under the Newlands Act were given to the arid states for the construction of storage reservoirs and permanent irrigation works. The water thus made available was to be distributed to settlers under the water laws of the states.

In 1865 the frontier of agricultural settlement had reached the eastern part of Kansas and Nebraska, which was roughly the ninety-sixth meridian. By the seventies, lands were being taken up beyond the hundredth meridian, where rainfall was insufficient for farming by traditional methods. As the railroads pushed west, the emigrants followed the lines of steel. The first emigrants to the western farming frontier, which was then east of the Missouri, were native Americans. In the 1850s came the Germans, then the Irish, the Swedes, Norwegians, Danes, Russians, Poles, Basques, Italians, and Greeks. In the 1890s and in the twentieth century came small farmers from adjoining prairie states, which had been settled by these previous migrations.

Sparked by the railroads, speculators, state immigration bureaus, land offices, the geological survey, private individuals, and booster clubs, the land rush intensified. Still, the Homestead Act was not the success its supporters had hoped it would be. This was due to several reasons. Shortly after the act was passed, an amendment was voted down that would have limited the amount of land a man could acquire under the act, and a second amendment was also voted down that would have made it possible to acquire land only by actual settlement. This left the way open for exploitation and evasion of the law. Immense land grants to the railroads also invited a breach of the public trust. The Northern Pacific had been given 38,916,338 acres; the Atlantic and Pacific (Santa Fe), 9,878,352 acres. Other railroads were given comparable grants. In 1891 the Revision Act attempted to regulate the acquisition of vast tracts of land by individuals and corporations. This act repealed the Timber Culture Act, amended the Desert Land Act, and repealed the preemption law with the proviso that claims initiated before passage of the act could be perfected under the old laws, but it was several decades too late for such legislation.

The greatest disappointment to the agrarian reformers, like Horace Greeley, was the failure of great numbers of workers from the industrial cities to take advantage of free land. Westward migration did not increase during hard times. The poor in cities lacked the money to make the move across the Missouri, nor did they have the vitality or the initiative, and the workers lacked skill as farmers. Greeley had hoped the West would serve as a safety valve for the laboring man. Instead, the decades after the Civil War witnessed prolonged and bitter labor disputes in the industrial areas. Between 1862 and 1890, at a time when the population of the United States was increasing rapidly, only 372,659 homesteads were filed on. By 1900 the ratio of tenant farmers on the once free land was growing, and many of those who were credited with having proved up on their land had mortgaged it heavily. Nor did an increase in the number of homesteads filed on from 1900-1922 bring prosperity. In Montana, where the homestead boom reached its peak between 1910-1922 (when most of the good land had been taken), 93 million acres were filed on in the state, the greatest part in the eastern section where it was impossible to make a living by farming a small acreage.

But foreign or American, the homesteaders had this in common—optimism. Everyone expected to make a fortune, and each town that was platted was going to be a prosperous and fast-growing community. The railroads were not entirely to blame, nor were the speculators; the emigrants saw what they wanted to see. They were as eager for a bargain as a promoter. Land—the feel of it in a man's hand, chocolate brown and moist; fields of tasseled grain, orchards heavy with fruit, and gardens laden with squash and corn; the trickle of water over pebbles and the stirring of the breeze among the cottonwoods—this, a man could see and hear. He could say, "This land is mine." "The homestead," an early-day settler in Idaho explained, "was the pioneer's boon, his institution of self-realization. It gave him standing, a place in the sun, it was his security against life."

Arizona and New Mexico, except for a few areas along the river bottoms, remained predominantly stock-raising regions. Not until World War I did farmers invade that range in numbers. This was true of Nevada, too, and most of Wyoming. In 1885-1890 settlers poured into western Nebraska, but only a few thousand filed on Wyoming land. Often the grangers in Wyoming were small cattlemen trying to increase their herds.

The myth of fertility, advertised by the railroads, was compounded by nature, which provided periods of moisture that encouraged the settler to believe there would always be sufficient rain to grow crops. And if the rain slackened (so the settlers believed), dry land farming, developed in the prairie states, could circumvent the drought. So millions of acres of native grass were turned to the plow.

The homesteaders were abstemious, frugal, and small thinking, worshiping in clapboard churches blistered by the sun, "learning" their children in one-room schoolhouses with privies in the back. They wore bib overalls and trudged about with shovels over their shoulders and they rode plowhorses in from the fields. They aged in failure, and, forever, they remained alien to the land.

The cattlemen scorned the homesteaders and, understandably angry at the invasion of the public domain they had come to consider their own, tried political pressure to discourage them. When that failed, they sometimes resorted to violence. The land, the cattlemen insisted, was not suitable for farming, only for grazing. On the high plains of the Rockies, the soil was granular, dry, and patched with sand and clay. The native grass that dried like straw in the summer was nutritious, but fragile.

The complaints of the cattlemen were attributed to self-interest, and, while this was true, the cattlemen knew the West as the homesteaders did not. Only two groups—the Pueblo Indians of the Southwest and the Mormons—had been able to raise crops in the arid land, and then only at a subsistence level and with frequent disasters.

The Pueblo Indians, by means of irrigating canals, had grown corn and squash and cotton in the desert. In modern times the Mormons had utilized irrigation to create oases out of wasteland. These thrifty, hardworking, and dedicated members of the Church of Latter-day Saints had labored in the long valley of the Wasatch Mountains. Directed as missionaries by Brigham Young, they had jolted in their wagons south to the piñon plateaus and cactus-studded deserts of Arizona; to the natural springs and yellow-ochre meadows on the Old Spanish Trail from Santa Fe to California that later became Las Vegas; down to the violet-colored valleys of the Virgin River and north to the high country of the Lemhi in Idaho, where the land sweeps to snow-patched peaks. The obedient colonizers grubbed out mesquite and sagebrush, dug irrigating canals, built homes shaded by Lombardy poplars, grew grain, alfalfa, melons, sorghums, and cotton, and raised livestock and turkeys. Their dams washed out, they were plagued by grasshoppers and drought. The Indians drove off their stock, and the Gentiles fought them with force and legislation. Their strength lay in the very thing that antagonized their non-Mormon neighbors—their solidarity. This element was lacking among the average homesteaders. But the stories of the people themselves tell far better what happened than statistics or comment.

Rufus Jones was a homesteader, a carpenter who had a neat, little home in Iowa and who decided to migrate West when, in 1910, he heard that "the U.S.A. was betting a half section of dry land that you couldn't live on and make a living from it for three years." This was land that Jim Hill's Great Northern Railroad advertised as rich beyond belief. So Jones sold his home, packed his furniture, and bought a sulky plow, a corn planter, a hay rake, and a light harness. Jones did not know how to harness a team and even less about farming, but he loaded his wife and equipment on an emigrant freight car operated by the Great Northern at special rates, his destination eastern Montana. This was high plains country, the far horizons penciled by rimrocks. The soil was gumbo, rooted with sagebrush. Until the arrival of the homesteaders, the plains had provided grazing for cattle; but now wagon tracks wound through the sagebrush, and barbed wire enclosed the range.

The first year wasn't so bad. Jones pulled and burned sagebrush on ten acres to plant potatoes and Iowa corn. He dug a cellar with a pick and shovel and built a twelve-by-eighteen-foot shack and tried to dig a well, too, but at eighteen feet when he found no water, he gave up. Two feet down he struck old sagebrush roots, which didn't impress him at the time. Only later did he recall that the sagebrush must have been buried by drifting sand in time of drought. The lack of a well meant that Mrs. Jones had to haul water from the creek. She was pregnant, too, but didn't mention what she thought about being left alone when her husband went to the mountains to cut two thousand fenceposts.

Every week that first year it rained. "We thought we had found the finest place in the world," Jones wrote.

This, despite a mortgage on the homestead and the failure of the corn to mature because Iowa seed could not produce in the short growing season of the high plains.

The next year Jones planted more corn and oats. The war in Europe had created a demand for agricultural products, and farmers were prospering. Still, the Joneses had to depend on outside income. After Mrs. Jones had her baby, assisted by her husband since no doctor was available, she went to work teaching school.

The Joneses were luckier than many homesteaders because they had extra cash. They needed it. One summer when the oats had headed out and the corn was ten inches high, the sky blackened and, without warning, hail whipped across the earth like icy bullets. Within an hour the storm was over, but the oats were flattened and only stubs remained of the corn. In the winter the stock suffered from the cold and lack of water when the creeks froze. Jones knew little about horses or cows; his neighbors knew less than he did. Many of them lost cows from abortions or milk fever. The horses ate locoweed or they got fistulas from improperly adjusted harnesses. And the homesteader was never prepared for the cruel vagaries of the weather. On a December noon the thermometer might show seventy degrees and the sun would be shining; by four o'clock the temperature would drop to thirty-five degrees below zero, and a blizzard would be blowing from the north.

In 1918 Jones planted 120 acres of wheat and 40 acres of corn. That summer, it did not rain every Saturday. It did not rain at all. The creek dried to a slimy puddle. The wheat shriveled, and the corn rattled like paper in the dry, hot wind. Dust, filtering through the cracks of the wooden shack, filmed the cookstove, the oilcloth-covered table, and the spreads on the iron bedstead.

The homesteaders stood in their doorways watching the sky and hoping for rain, but all they saw was the dust that the wind swirled from the plowed fields.

Two years later, the price of wheat went down.

Rufus Jones was a man who lacked the ability to express himself. A more eloquent description of homesteading (this time in Idaho) was given to us by a woman called Annie Pike Greenwood, who was the daughter of a prosperous business-man in Kansas City and whose husband was an educated, upper-class man of German extraction. Mr. Greenwood loved the land and the great outdoors and when he read a magazine article describing the West as the fulfillment of an agrarian dream, he gave up his position, bought wagons, a team, a cow, and agricultural implements and moved with Annie to southeastern Idaho.

". . . nothing but sagebrush, as far as eye could see . . . no tree, no green."

This was, indeed, arid country where volcanic ash mingled with the clay and sand. "Water was money." The Mormons had been the first settlers who "trusting the Lord and the work of their own hands," had prospered. They had been the only ones who had.

In the beginning Annie imagined herself as a pioneer on the western frontier, but her enthusiasm did not last. No imagination could cancel reality—the unceasing wind and the dust that greyed the clothes and gritted the food; the bedbugs and the pack rats and the flies blackening the freshly butchered meat. In the summer the heat drained the strength from a woman's body and, in the winter, she shivered in the cold that no amount of sagebrush roots shoved into the stove could keep out of the tar-paper shack. Worst of all was the "terrible forced labor, no rest, no money." As long as a woman could work, she was useful. Butchering and cultivating the crops was up to the men, everything else, including helping with the harvest, was women's work. One of Annie's neighbors rode a rake when she was far advanced in pregnancy, a baby less than two years old clinging to her lap.

The women bore their children without a doctor, bedded on dirty blankets, assisted by a neighbor. Some of them died of septicemia or abortions. Some committed suicide, and some just gave up and died.

"I learned," Annie wrote, "that out in the brush folks are not greatly impressed by anything but how much money you got for that hog. How can you blame them? The farmer gives his very life, and the lives of his family to raise a hog. The hog means reality to him."

Annie feared what was happening to her, and she worried about the future of her children in an environment that deprived them of books and music and the amenities of life. She was afraid her children might become like the boys and girls she taught in the one-room school who smoked and chewed and were exposed to brutality and sexual perversion of the worst kind. Yet Annie was not repulsed by her students, she was saddened by a great pity, and it was this pity that inspired her to buy some phonograph records and invite parents and children to a party. When the music filled the one-room schoolhouse, the children and the men and women listened motionless and in silence. "These farm people had felt so much, had suffered so much; had suppressed so much of joyous desire."

In the end the Greenwoods lost their homestead, as did most of the other farmers. "Sold at auction" became a common phrase. Rufus Jones and his family could not make a living on their land, either, so they left eastern Montana and moved to a town where carpentry proved more profitable than potatoes. Finally, all over the West the dust drifted into deserted tar-paper shacks and against fence posts tangled with rusty wire. The dust blew from the fields that had once been open range, where the grass roots and the sagebrush had held the soil. But the grass did not return. The plow had cut too deeply.

The homesteaders' shacks, like the ghost towns of the gold rush, remained as mute reminders of the fallacy of one more western myth.

During World War II the homesteaders and their children moved to Seattle to work for Boeing or to Los Angeles to work for Lockheed. After the war they also moved in-state to towns, making them metropolitan statistical centers. Members of farming communities, like members of cowtowns, became old-age pensioners of the cities, resigned to sitting on the Interstate like inhabitants of rest homes, watching the world go by.

In the 1970s a Department of Agriculture report stated that the trend would be toward even larger and fewer farms; as many as one-third to one-half of the farms presently listed would no longer be in production at the end of the 1970s. Great changes would occur in what was called the "economics of capital management," and mechanization would continue to replace labor.

In regard to labor, the farmer as well as the rancher has ceased to rely on hired men. On one farm the irrigators are all old, and the manager—knowing he cannot replace them with younger hands—has purchased huge machines that propel themselves along a ditch under their own power, spraying water as they go. But these machines cost a great deal of money and the little man cannot afford to buy them.

Yet the agrarian myth will not die. Recently, a former assistant director of the Office of Economic Opportunity declared that the solution to our overcrowded cities lay in the 400 million idle acres of the public domain. The former administrator recommended that a study be made of the hundreds of millions of acres (mostly desert in the West) to see if what he called "income producing units" of industrial, commercial, and agricultural activity might not be relocated from urban areas to this sparsely populated region. Land would be sold at present-day prices to the poor and to industries that would hire the poor so that the underprivileged of the nation would have "a vested interest in America." Immense technological advances in transportation, farming techniques, irrigation, desalinization processes, and speed of shipping products would, the administrator felt, make the program possible.

Perhaps this is the pattern of the future. A hundred years ago that was what Horace Greeley had hoped for his agrarian utopia.

Lo, the Poor Indian!

VI

Like the figures on a psychedelic poster, the Indians have been garishly colored and blown up larger than life. One poster represents the civil rights version of a noble minority persecuted by the dominant whites; the other poster depicts a savage scalping an emigrant kneeling in prayer. Both posters are extremes designed for public consumption.

The westerner today is supposed to be obsessed by guilt because of his ancestors' injustice to the Indians. The truth is that the average westerner feels no guilt whatsoever about the Indians. Indeed, he hardly thinks about them, and those who do have not grown noticeably more tolerant.

A well-to-do rancher described a member of a tribe recently as a "dirty, greasy Indian."

As it happened, the Indian was trying to institute reforms on the reservation that would have conflicted with the interests of the rancher, but the Indian was not only thinking of his people; he hoped to benefit financially from the reforms.

"Drunks" is a common adjective applied to the Indians by westerners, also "lazy" and "dishonest." These are terms that in many cases are deserved, but they apply to local whites as well.

Failure to recognize the Indians' faults is to do them a disservice. The Indians are not the noble red men, they are human beings like the rest of us, and it is with this in mind that we should recognize why they drink, why they do not hold a job, and why they are jailed.

The Indians are emerging into a technological world as an underprivileged minority. They are like patients learning to walk after a long illness. Dependence on the federal government has atrophied their initiative and self-respect; the traditions that kept their spirits flickering in the endless night have separated white man from red. For a hundred years the Indians lived in isolation on reservations, most of which are located in the Rocky Mountain West. As a child, I grew up knowing that if I saw a particularly desolate and isolated part of the country, it was a reservation. I was familiar, too, with the sight of Indian women in moccasins and shawls wrapped about their shoulders, digging for scraps in garbage cans.

James Farmer, one of the founders of the Congress of Racial Equality, said, "The Indian is worse off than the Negro. . . . Their annual wage is even lower than the average Negro's."

Miss Indian America for 1968 said, "The Indian must regain his pride in his past and have determination to make a better future for himself."

Myth has handicapped the Indians and the worst offenders in this respect are novelists and television script writers, although the idealists in their audience are partly to blame. The idealists can be stubborn, as were our foreign friends who confessed to us that their greatest wish in coming to America was to see an Indian in buckskins and feathers. We tried to tell our friends that the Indians no longer wore buckskins or lived in tipis, but they insisted on seeing "real" Indians. One day a battered car roared past; at the wheel was a fellow with pockmarked skin and a mod haircut. Later in the day, we waited at a grocery stand while the woman ahead of us bought a pack of beer. The woman wore tight jeans and a skimpy blouse and her hair was puffed high on her head.

The woman and the fellow in the car were Indians, but I did not tell our friends; they treasured their mythical figures too dearly to relinquish them.

Even the Indians tend to view themselves within the context of legend, which makes it difficult for them to know if they are nomadic aborigines or citizens of twentieth-century America.

Civil rights people who would have the white man confess his guilt fail to consider Indian-white relations within the context of a nineteenth-century environment. This was a time when men were still hanged publicly in England, and the theory of evolution was described as heretical. The whites were not the only race that claimed superiority; the Chinese and Japanese considered the Caucasians barbarians, and the Indians themselves tolerated the whites until they were overwhelmed by their numbers.

From a practical point of view, it must be admitted that the Indians were Stone Age nomads who roamed a sparsely populated land rich in resources. This land was necessary to the development of a great nation. The tragedy of the Indians was their encounter not with the white race, but with the Industrial Age.

Our Indian policy permitted outrages that blackened American history; however, many of the injustices were not perpetuated as deliberate genocide, but with the desire to benefit the Indians. Others were committed out of ignorance.

Our custom of making treaties with the tribes as though they had been sovereign nations was an example of our ineptness—a practice that, after the Civil War, contributed to the final tragedy. In the late 1860s government relations with the Indians were dominated by humanitarians who before and during the war had been ardent abolitionists; some of them were members of the Reform Movement, which advocated free land as a panacea to all ills. The humanitarians accomplished a great deal of good—if it had not been for their outcries, the fate of the Indians would have been left to the westerners who favored extermination—but unfortunately the humanitarians, for all their devotion to the Indians' cause, were remarkably ignorant of the western tribes whom they pictured as noble red men. Also, as George Hyde, authority on the Sioux, wrote, "Their Indian policy was not based on consideration as to what the Indians desired but on their own views as to what would be best for the Indians."

We still have the same sort of well-meaning people in the mid-twentieth century; we have them all over the world, but in foreign lands the local government can expel do-gooders. The Indians have not had that privilege, and today they are finally making their wishes known—Indians want to manage their own affairs without interference from church groups, benevolent societies, government bureaus, anthropologists, or historians.

The so-called "Peace Movement" of the late 1860s illustrates how government policy with the best intentions led to disaster. In Arizona emissaries from Washington made "peace treaties" with the Apaches who had terrorized the Southwest for hundreds of years, and, in the north, with the Sioux and Cheyenne who had harassed settlers along the Oregon Trail. The emissaries could not understand that a few friendly hangers-on could not sign for the hostiles or that war was a way of life among the Indians; that warriors were the leaders of the people and that status was won by the plunder of enemies. Nor did the Indians understand that promises made by the emissaries might not be kept or that expected presents would not always arrive.

Both Indians and the Great White Father in Washington underestimated the advancing tide of emigrants who were determined to acquire land and the riches of the West and who would not tolerate the interference of "cruel, bloodthirsty, and treacherous savages."

The humanitarians, to give them credit, did attempt to impress the Indians with the futility of fighting by sending a selected number of chiefs to Washington. The idea was sound, but again an inspiration that was better in theory than reality. The Indians who were left at home refused to believe the stories their chiefs told them upon their return. Nor did the eastern visits go according to plan, as in the case of a chief who startled the audience at Cooper Union in New York by saying, "When the Great Father first sent out men to our people I was poor and thin; now I am large and fat. That is because I have been stuffed full with their lies."

Too much emphasis has been placed on the military defeat of the Indians, which ensued in Arizona after the failure of the Peace Policy and in the north following the winter campaigns of Generals Miles and Crook that came after the temporary victory of the Indians at the Little Big Horn. The greatest damage done the Indians was not through the wounds they received in battle with the military, but the destruction of their identity by the white man's society that was accomplished on the reservations.

By 1886 nearly all the tribes in the Rocky Mountain West were confined to areas designated by the government. In 1887 the Dawes Act, instigated by humanitarians, was passed by Congress. This Act authorized the President to parcel tribal lands to individual members so they could plow and plant crops. Surplus land was to be purchased under the authority of the Secretary of the Interior and the money put into a fund to civilize and educate the tribes. In theory the Act sounded feasible; it was an honest attempt to help the Indians become self-supporting, but it failed because it did not take into consideration the fact that the Indians were not ready to become farmers. The customs and habits of centuries could not be shed within months. Most of the surplus land passed into ownership by whites who had supported the humanitarians for purposes of their own. The majority of the humanitarians were honest men who had no idea of the reason for the support of the speculators, businessmen, and ranchers who profited from government contracts. The more Indians who had to be fed, clothed, and housed, the fatter the contracts; and the more Indians who were moved to reservations, the more land available for speculation.

When drought ruined what few crops the Indians had planted and the beef herds delivered to the reservation proved insufficient to prevent hunger (because of white corruption), the Indians protested to the agents, but the protests were unheeded. Refusing to admit the failure of their plan, the humanitarians blamed the chiefs whom they termed "nonprogressive." As a result, the humanitarians saw that instructions were issued to the agents to break the power of the chiefs although the chiefs were the only leaders the Indians were willing to accept or were capable of understanding.

Continued drought, cuts in the beef rations, and the spread of disease among a nomadic people forced to remain in one place brought increased hardship. "They were starving and their children were dying, but no one in the white man's land seemed to know it or care."

After one last, ill-fated uprising on the northern reservations, the Ghost Dance Rebellion, the Indians accepted the inevitable and the long night fell for all the western tribes.

The Indians became the dispossessed, the poor minority, and because they were no longer hostile, and, therefore, not in the news, and because the Spanish American War and World War I focussed attention outside our national boundaries, the Indians also became a forgotten people whose welfare was dominated by the Bureau of Indian Affairs and through the Bureau by agents who exercised a great deal of power. Few jobs were available on the reservations, which necessitated the Indians living on a system similar to a dole. Scorned by whites, their old traditions and pride destroyed, subject to the petty tyrannies of the agents, they existed in a state of hopeless misery.

In 1924 the government in a burst of generosity made the Indians American citizens, but it was not until 1934 that the mistakes of the Dawes Act were admitted and legislation passed to remedy it. This was the Wheeler-Howard Act that sought to encourage self-government among the Indians and preserve their culture. Allotments of tribal land were also stopped, but too late to prevent a large amount of the most fertile land from passing into white ownership. The Wheeler-Howard Act was a step toward alleviating the plight of the Indians, but was interrupted by World War II; young Indians and Bureau of Indian Affairs personnel, who might have implemented the Act, volunteered for military service. The Bureau budget was cut, and roads, buildings, and schools on the reservations were allowed to deteriorate. After the war another attempt was made to help the Indians by the passage of the Indian Claims Commission Act in 1946, which awarded damages to tribes for lands they had been forced to sell too cheaply or that had been unjustly confiscated.

Money paid out by the Claims Commission (and it has run into the millions) was too late to help the Indians who had actually suffered the most from past injustices. The Flathead woman, whose funeral we attended in the early 1960s, was a victim of such wrongs. All her life the woman had lived in a log cabin on the reservation. When she was buried, services were held in a little church that had been built by priests when the Flatheads, against their will, were moved from their ancestral home in the Bitterroot Valley to a reservation farther north. The funeral was held on a winter day. As we entered the church, I saw the cemetery, snow-blown among the weeds, surrounded by a broken fence. Inside faded plastic flowers decorated the altar where the mortician fidgeted, impatient of a delay in what was to him routine business.

For a day and a night the Indians had held a wake in the home of the dead woman to which only Indians had been invited. Now the woman lay in a closed coffin before the altar, and we were told she wore her buckskin dress. In the first rows sat her contemporaries: a few old women wearing shawls, colored bandannas, and rubbers over their moccasins; and men with grey braids and checked shirts. One who was blind lifted his sightless eyes to the altar and, when the priest finished speaking, the old Indians began to chant the Lord's Prayer in Salish. As I listened to the thin, ancient voices in that little church among the plastic flowers, I wept unashamed and I saw other people were crying too—not from guilt; it was too late for that—but because of the pity of it all.

And yet we should not always associate tragedy with the Indians, for they are not a sombre or a stoic people by nature. They laugh a great deal among themselves and have a sense of humor. My husband tells a story of a trip through Wyoming during the days of the C.C.C. (Civilian Conservation Corps) when he stopped at a café near the Shoshoni Reservation. As he got out of the car, he noticed a group of tourists surrounding a big, good-looking Indian in a black Stetson.

One of the tourists was saying, "Do you speak English?"

The Indian grunted, "No speakum English."

Delighted by this proof of savagery, the tourists, after snapping pictures, departed, whereupon the Indian turned around to my husband who was in uniform and said in educated accents, "Good morning, lieutenant, what can I do for you?"

Indians are generous, too; they share with each other and with friends. Among our most treasured possessions are beaded bags and moccasins given to us by the Indians. But one of the most delightful traits of the Indians is their lack of pomposity and their skill at pricking this trait in the white man, as was evidenced not long ago when a dam, built by a power company on a site leased from the Indians, was dedicated with much formality. Speaker after speaker, all white, extolled the Power Company with frequent references to the United States and God and how much the Power Company was benefitting the Indians by their payments to the tribe.

At last Chief Charlo was called on to speak. He uttered a few words in the Salish language and then sat down. His interpreter translated, "We heard a lot from the Power Company about how much they were going to pay us for the dam. So far, we haven't seen a cent of the money."

Charlo was the last of the hereditary chiefs of the Flatheads, a reservation Indian. There are still many reservation Indians, and they are inclined to distrust the Indians who adopt the ways of the white man. In turn, both distrust and are distrusted by the new Indian militants who remain a minority.

The more isolated the reservation, the greater the distrust of the old-style Indian for the new. Added to this is the suspicion between tribes. In historical times the Indians fought more often with each other than with the whites. This is true today in a modified form, although it is being minimized by such organizations as the Congress of American Indians.

A government report in the late 1960s listed 50,000 Indians of a total Indian population of 552,000 living in shacks and cabins without sanitary facilities; fifty percent of Indian children dropped out before completing high school, and unemployment was more than ten times the national average, while Indians held one of the highest rates in the nation for sickness, suicide, and alcoholism.

Assimilation and migration to the cities have not proved to be the solution; too many Indians are unprepared for urban life and are untrained for jobs, so that instead of bettering themselves, they sink to welfare in the ghettos. Essentially, the Indian problem is a rural one, while that of the black is urban, a fact frequently misunderstood by urban-oriented liberals and politicians. Each tribe on each reservation deals with its problems in its own way, and varied as the people and location are, a general pattern emerges.

The Indians are taking an increasingly active part in their own affairs. One example was the Governor of Tusuque Pueblo in 1969. When we were in Santa Fe, we drove to nearby Tusuque to talk to the official. Tusuque, like the capital of New Mexico, is on a high, volcanic plateau that is rough, arid, and slashed with sandy arroyos and darkened by piñon pines. In 1969, Tusuque consisted of a clutter of separate, flat-topped adobe houses, an adobe church, and a school. Many houses had the old, round-topped clay oven in the back yard. Power lines and wires testified to electricity, but despite this evidence of the twentieth century, the community did not look prosperous. The few fields were badly cultivated, the adobe was scaling from the walls of the houses, and a building that was once a general store was boarded up.

The Governor of the Pueblo was a contrast to the community: he was young, round faced, inclined to plumpness— the epitome of a modern, dynamic executive. When I had phoned for an interview, he told me he could only give me half an hour; while we were talking, we were interrupted twice, once by a telephone call and once by a visitor at the door. The house was a modern, one-story home with a television set in the living room, and on the wall was the cane that had been the Governor's badge of office for centuries.

The Governor was willing to talk, but he was distracted. He was deeply involved in politics and business, as we knew. The day before we had heard him speak at the dedication ceremonies of the Northern Pueblos Agency, which had recently been established by the Bureau of Indian Affairs, although a report extremely critical of the B.I.A.'s "empire building" and "paternalism" had just been made public in Washington.

The Governor told us that he was trying to persuade a real estate firm to develop the Pueblo lands.

"We got no minerals or big ranches," he explained. Unlike the plains tribes who had received lands from the U.S. government, the Pueblo Indians had received theirs as Spanish land grants. The Governor was proud of this and of the Pueblo system of government that had survived through the centuries. Indeed, my impression was that the Pueblo Indians considered their culture unique among the Indians.

Over the years the Pueblo lands had been whittled down to small tracts, so the only possible source of income, as the Governor could see it, was in real estate development.

"What about termination?" I asked.

"Indians should keep their reservations for the forseeable future," the Governor said. "After that, I dunno."

The majority of Indians would have expressed greater interest in retaining their reservations, but the Governor's attitude could have been explained by the limited income potential of the Pueblo lands. Most of the young people worked in Sante Fe, and even the old men and women commuted to the Plaza or the Hotel La Fonda where they squatted against the wall, a blanket spread in front of them on which turquoise and silver jewelry manufactured in Hong Kong were displayed.

The Navajos, too, are assuming more responsibility for their own welfare, but they differ from the Pueblo Indians in that they are not close to a city. They exemplify the tribes who value their reservation and who are developing it to provide job opportunities and better living conditions for the people. This is an important general trend among the Indians who own millions of acres that can produce cattle, minerals, and timber, and that can be exploited for tourism.

The Navajos own oil wells and have developed a cattle industry that threatens to make traditional sheep raising obsolete; they cut timber and finish it in one of the most modern sawmills in the Southwest, mine coal by the newest methods, and do a booming tourist business. There is even a Navajo College and, in the tribal headquarters at Window Rock, an IBM computer. The offices of the Bureau of Indian Affairs are also at Window Rock, and much of the development of the reservation has been due to B.I.A. officials and white corporations, but the Navajos are taking over more jobs as they become qualified.

Roger Tsoie is representative of the progressive young Navajo. The last time we were in Arizona, Roger was a ranger at Monument Valley, which is owned by the Navajo tribe. When a representative of the Golden Sands Tour Company drove me around the valley, he invited Roger to accompany us. We picked Roger up at the modern stone and glass ranger building that overlooks the fluted, cinnamon-red columns called the Mittins. Roger proved to be a good-looking boy with close-cropped black hair. He might well have posed as a model in his ranger uniform of black western hat, western boots, and the insignia of the Navajo Rangers on his sleeve. At first he was reticent, but as we drove past immense red cliffs and sand dunes, he became more talkative. When I asked him where he'd gotten his ranger training, he told us at Window Rock and explained that he had two years of college at the University of Arkansas on a government program that sponsors Indian students. There are many such programs; the problem is not to find funds but students to take advantage of them.

Until he was eleven, Roger said, he'd been kept out of school to tend sheep. However, his parents wanted him to get an education, so he was sent to a Navajo school in Los Angeles. He was in the city for seven years working part time. But he did not like urban life, many Indians do not, so he returned to the reservation.

"It's important," Roger said, "if your parents want you to go to school." Many Indian parents do not want their children to get a high school or college education, because they are afraid the children will leave their homes; and if their children do get jobs in cities, they will not make enough to help the old people.

In a shallow plain surrounded by rose-red mesas, we saw a hogan and a little girl tending sheep. The scene was staged for tourists.

"Young people don't like to tend sheep any more," said Elsie Begaii, a Navajo official at the B.I.A. headquarters in Window Rock.

Nor are the young women interested in weaving the magnificent rugs that have been so long valued in the West. Weaving demands time and patience and has to be done in the isolation of the home, and is not as remunerative as white man's wages. The same applies to the silver jewelry that is made by the men, and indeed to native crafts on every western reservation. Periodically, efforts are made to encourage the manufacture and sale of such crafts on the reservations in the hope of aiding the Indians, but these efforts are as effective as setting up a cobbler in competition with a chain store shoe business. Actually, the trading posts and souvenir shops dominated by the whites profited the most from Indian crafts. The Indians are just beginning to make money for themselves in the sale of moccasins and jewelry—even though they are made in Hong Kong.

The Apaches are another tribe who are developing their reservation, but their land does not have the minerals that the Navajo reservation does; and the Apaches are not as sophisticated as their cousins. The Apache reservation is in east central Arizona where ledges of volcanic rock form the Mogollon Rim. This is high country of pine, swampy meadows, and quaking aspen. Farther west, the land drops to semi-desert slashed by canyons and broken by cactus-studded hills. As we drove along a nearly deserted road in early spring, we saw wooden shacks in remote clearings, junk automobiles, and brush wickiups. A woman wearing a long, old fashioned skirt did not glance up as we passed. At the agency I encountered the same indifference when a sullen, muscular young man shoved past me on the steps without appearing to notice that I was there. His black hair was cut in bangs above fierce black eyes. I could not help thinking—that is what the old, predatory Apache looked like.

Yet the Apaches are struggling to adjust to the modern world. At McNary, a sawmill town, we saw teenagers with mod haircuts playing pinball machines in a café, and girls and boys giggling over cokes, as they do everywhere else in the United States. The high school was playing football and a beauty pageant was being staged to select a queen.

On an economic level the tribe, aided by a two-million-dollar government loan, established the Fort Apache Timber Company, where more than 200 Apaches are employed by the company at $2.50 an hour. All profits go to the tribe. Studies are being made of mineral resources such as iron, copper, and silica, and the tribe owns one of the finest herds of Herefords in Arizona. The Apaches enjoy racing over rough country after the cattle and shouting in the dust, but they are not as efficient on the business end; nor do they excel at meeting tourists. Tourism is being developed with the construction of campgrounds and artificial lakes and the sale of hunting and fishing permits, although to date the surrounding white-owned motels and souvenir shops seem to be profiting more from the tourists than are the Apaches.

At the Agency I asked a Bureau of Indian Affairs official about the Indians taking over their own affairs.

The official perspired profusely and chain smoked. "If they think they can go it alone, let them try."

The official's job, and that of thousands more in the B.I.A. are endangered by the Indian demand for more autonomy.

The B.I.A. official was not as optimistic about the

progress of the Apaches as government people had been at other reservations.

"Progress? Women used to ride in the back of the pickups, now they drive them."

A newly constructed motel on the reservation was closed because no Apaches were capable of operating it. At the same time I noticed that the Indian boarding school operated by the B.I.A. at Fort Apache that had once been a frontier army post, would have been condemned by a white community. Bricks crumbled from the buildings, the paint peeled from doors and window sashes; the grounds were overgrown with weeds; two Indian children played listlessly with a baseball on the cracked concrete of what had once been a tennis court.

Under so-called remedial and welfare programs, one Indian child in four is taken from his reservation home and sent off to boarding schools or to a foster home. Recently, this policy has been criticized. "Boarding schools," said Dr. Daniel J. O'Connell, consultant in psychiatry of the Harvard School of Public Health, "are operated by the government for disturbed children with behavior problems, or for children from disrupted families, but they are really homes of detention, with no rehabilitation services at all."

The Indian children who attend public schools have problems too. The Indian culture is ignored, and many youngsters start with the handicap of not knowing English. Often the boys and girls are ashamed of their poor teeth, bad skins, and old clothes, and in some areas encounter racial discrimination.

After nearly a hundred years of being responsible for the Indians, the Bureau of Indian Affairs does not seem to have accomplished as much as it might have. Charges of empire building and paternalism have some basis in fact. On the other hand, the Bureau has been handicapped by lack of funds and plagued by politics. Pressure groups influence Indian legislation, and the humanitarians are still busy. Many people who are well informed and genuinely concerned are working for programs to aid the Indians, but others are modern counterparts of the humanitarians of the last century who did so much damage. In the B.I.A., as in any government department, there are some people who are not as capable as they might be; there are also experienced and dedicated men and women who are doing their best to help the Indians.

Progress might seem slow to the militants—and it has been slow—but the pace is accelerating. In 1967 federal agencies other than the Bureau of Indian Affairs spent more than $193 million on various programs from which the Indians benefited directly.

One program at the University of Montana in 1968-1969, funded by the Bureau of Indian Affairs, the Manpower Development and Training Administration, and the Office of Economic Opportunity, provided for the basic education of Indian families who had been living on reservations. While the men were trained in basic skills and prevocational studies, the women were given help in the preparation of budgets, nutrition, cooking, and sanitation. Older children were sent to public schools, the younger ones to kindergartens. The programs had the expected high rate of dropouts, but many of those who dropped out wanted to return; the majority of them had been high school dropouts before they entered the program.

"We have seen a great change in how they feel about themselves," said Dr. Allen Pope, director of the project, referring to the Indians. "They now know that they are successful people."

"The Indians need more lawyers," an Indian friend who was attending the University of Chicago Law School on a scholarship told me. "They need public relations men, educators, teachers."

"What do the Indians want?" I asked.

"They are asking for development of tribal lands, for more and better education, for help in relocation off reservations, for education of tribal council officials, for improved housing and preservation of their cultural heritage, and especially for Indians to have a greater say in Indian affairs. Above all, they want to be able to stand up and say proudly, 'I am an Indian!' "

Slightly Higher
West of the Rockies

VII

A cartoon in a national magazine showed a couple driving toward a towering range of mountains, and the wife saying to her husband, "No wonder prices are slightly higher west of the Rockies."

The cartoon was amusing; in another way it was not so funny, for it pinpointed the economic realities of the Rocky Mountain West. In the nineteenth century the emigrant saw only the myth that depicted the West as a self-sufficient area where miners washed nuggets from streams and where cattle and timber barons bestrode the land like giants. Believing that a fortune lay beyond those mountains, the emigrants abandoned their homes for an unknown wilderness. If their

hopes had not been so great, they would not have endured
the agonies of the Oregon and Santa Fe trails. Economic reality has seldom inspired a nation.

Today, the myth altered to the late twentieth century
still draws people to the Rocky Mountain West. In the past,
the emigrants bought a wagon and oxen and started across
the Missouri, or they traveled by stagecoach or by train and
they were usually motivated by rumor. In modern times,
many of them write, before they decide on the move, to a
State Employment Agency about job possibilities. These state
officials reply to the job seekers in various ways. Some send a
letter describing the climate and opportunities. Almost all try
to discourage people from moving to the Rocky Mountain
region to find work. New industry is eagerly sought, but
twentieth-century emigrants who need work or part-time
work are not wanted in a region that cannot support them.

Such a region is northwestern Montana, a country where
forests envelop mountains in claustrophobic gloom. What
timber is not owned by a large corporation is owned by the
federal government, and the majority of jobs available are in
construction, or logging, or, if a man wants to be independent, cutting Christmas trees. The region was one of the last
in the United States to have electricity and the shacks that
are glimpsed at long intervals are smothered by black firs;
they are the western equivalent of poor-white habitations in
other parts of the nation. A man will not starve; he can always kill a deer, but he becomes eroded by poverty and
loneliness and, if he has little education, his recreation centers
on whiskey and women. On a crossroads in this region is a
one-room, clapboard saloon called the Dirty Shame, and
here, one Sunday morning, we heard a fellow tell the following story. The fellow, in company with half a dozen companions in loggers' boots and jeans, was drinking beer with

whiskey chasers.

"Did you hear what happened to Jim? He figgered he could do better if he cut his Christmas trees and hauled them himself to Los Angeles. You know that old two-ton Chevy he's got? Well, he and another guy started cutting in October and by December they had a pretty good load. They got to Los Angeles—which is more'n I thought they'd do with that truck—and Jim says, 'Let's have a couple of drinks and then sell the trees.' Christ, they really tied one on. When they come to, it was bright daylight and Jim staggered outa bed and says to the other guy, 'Well, I guess we better sell them trees.' So they drove to the nearest wholesale lot and told the guy that owned it they had the best load of Christmas trees that ever come to Los Angeles. The guy like to burst, 'Are you guys crazy! Do you know what day this is? It's the twenty-sixth of December!' "

Loud guffaws from the assembled company greeted the story. In a country where existence is marginal, humor can be cruel.

Similar stories could be repeated to illustrate economic ventures in the poorer regions of the Rocky Mountain West.

Chambers of commerce and state industrial agencies do not like these stories. They prefer to tell about Mr. Robert Hansberger, president of Boise Cascade in Idaho, who was profiled in the *New York Times* financial section. Under Mr. Hansberger's leadership Boise Cascade grew from a regional lumber company to a national concern, with interests in paper, packaging, building products, and urban-renewal projects.

Mr. Hansberger said, "To sustain this kind of growth, a company must attract and motivate people. We think that Idaho, with its abundant beauty and the richness of family life it offers, has been a compelling influence in our ability to achieve that purpose. There is something about the bigness of the land that convinces people there are no limits to the boundaries of imagination, initiative, and personal growth."

Stories similar to that of Boise Cascade could be repeated elsewhere in the Rocky Mountain West, especially in Colorado, Utah, Arizona, and New Mexico, states that have shown amazing prosperity in the 1960s; but it would be safe to assume that there are still more Christmas-tree cutters than officials of a Boise Cascade in the Rocky Mountain region.

The phenomenal growth statistics since World War II do not reflect the whole picture. On the plus side, the West of 1970 is as different from the West of 1945 as the West of the fur trade differed from the West of the gold camps. We are told the region will experience even greater change in the technological age that is replacing the industrial era. The West, like the nation, is in a period of transition that began after World War II when the West witnessed a rapid increase in modern, paved highways and air traffic, as well as metropolitan statistical areas such as "oasis" cities of Salt Lake, Denver, and Phoenix. In the Southwest, the swinging, noisy, gaudy influence of southern California has routed the slow tempo of the Indian-Spanish culture. Sun City. London Bridge imported to the desert. Holiday Inns. Pink plastic flags fluttering above miles of used car lots, new service and manufacturing industries. Defense plants. The whine of jets from countless air bases. Multimillion-dollar dams.

Yet between the neon signs exist empty deserts and high plateaus where the wind blows across the sage, and small towns that are bypassed by the Interstate so that the occupants of the speeding cars cannot see the boarded-up windows and the old men reminiscing in the general store that sells stale Hershey bars and canned goods to a dwindling rural population.

The Rocky Mountain states share in common certain factors that create their economic problems, some to a greater and some to a lesser degree. The first of these factors is geographical location. The West is isolated from markets in the East and on the West Coast, so that even today, with the competition of railroads, air lines, and trucking firms, the Rocky Mountain region remains a "high cost" area with regard to transportation and distribution. What this simply means is that it costs more to go from Idaho to New York than it does to go from New York to London. One of the reasons for the growth of Denver and Salt Lake City is that these cities are the most strategically located in the West for east-west and north-south traffic.

Transportation costs discourage industry, and industry, we are told, tends to locate close to other industries, which explains the growth of population centers. Markets are a factor in the location of industry, too, and in new investment, which is influenced by the advantages and disadvantages of other areas.

Since 1920 regions in which manufacturing and service activities predominate have had higher incomes than those regions where agriculture and mining were the main income producers. This was the case in the West, and still is, with the exception of Arizona, Utah, and Colorado. Except for the brief period from 1880 to 1900—when personal income in the northern Rocky Mountain region was among the highest in the nation, due mainly to mining and the scarcity of population—the per capita income in the West, excluding Nevada, has been below the national average. The 1963-1966 United States Department of Commerce figures are typical; they show only slight variations over the last thirty years. Of the states in the northern Rocky Mountain area in 1966, Colorado had the highest per capita income of $2,872, which was still below the national average of $2,940. Arizona ranked slightly higher than New Mexico, but still below the national average; while Nevada ranked above all the other states and above the national average because of Las Vegas and Reno. However, in 1967 Colorado's per capita income increased to $3,432, which was above the national average. Arizona's figures might have been low because of the large Indian population.

An encouraging note was that from 1963 to 1966 per capita income in all eight states in the Rocky Mountain area increased. Colorado, Utah, and the Southwest are listed as areas where income will rise with future growth in population. These are states where manufacturing has become a major income producer.

The affluence of one of these areas was recently impressed on me in Colorado Springs. My husband and I were invited to dinner in the Broadmore Hotel, which was built with mining money in the era of large, luxurious hostelries and which, unlike many of its counterparts, has been modernized with a new wing that contains a dining room aglitter with crystal chandeliers. The food and the service were superb; while we ate smoked salmon, tournedos, and strawberries out of season, we could see from the window the city lights cascading down the mountains to the prairie, the lights of Fort Carson, and those of NORAD (Air Defense Command). Out of sight to the north was the Air Force Academy with its many-spired, glass-roofed chapel. In the lobby of the Broadmore we encountered skiiers bound for Aspen and Vail, government experts from Washington, business officials specializing in defense contracts, a famous writer, and a scientist of world renown. Our host was a rancher-banker who told us, "Our industries, here, are limited to aerospace and electronics."

Denver is an affluent city, too, with its many-storied Hilton Hotel, often used for conventions, and with an area of the old town that has been restored to red-brick specialty shops and restaurants. Phoenix is also synonymous with money; sprawled across the arid valley, it boasts of luxurious inns with palm-bordered swimming pools and an I. Magnin store. Like the Hilton Hotels, I. Magnin stores are only located in growth areas.

Albuquerque and Salt Lake, Las Vegas and Reno are enclaves of wealth that, by contrast, make the uninhabitated miles and the small towns seem even lonelier and shabbier than they are. The lifeblood is drained from the rural areas to the metropolitan centers. In the cowtowns and the mining communities, the family-owned grocery has been replaced by the supermarket in a larger trading center; while this is true of the United States as a whole, it is more visible in the West because there is so much empty land between cities.

The land is another common factor in the West that creates its economic problems. Much of it is submarginal, and what is tillable is dependent on irrigation because of the aridity of the climate. To understand what this means, you should see the San Rafael Desert in Utah that resembles a partially incinerated carcass, with hills like ribs protruding from grey ash. Or the plateaus of Wyoming at the end of summer, sun-parched, where cattle huddle around the water tanks. Or you should walk through the forests in a dry season when the underbrush cracks like glass and the smell of pitch is in the air, hot and explosive.

And, then you should see water seeping from an irrigation ditch across earth dehydrated to clay-colored lumps by drought; see how the soil darkens with moisture and softens, as a recalcitrant child to the love of a mother's arms.

The green of alfalfa in the river bottoms, the palm trees in Phoenix, and the cotton fields and pecan orchards near

Tucson are made possible by irrigation. Indeed, this is the case with the cities and the industries. Phoenix owes its existence to one of the first Bureau of Reclamation projects in the West—Roosevelt Dam on the Salt River, built in 1909. Since then billions of dollars in federal funds have been appropriated for hydroelectric and irrigation projects constructed by the Bureau of Reclamation or the Army Corps of Engineers. In 1969 $1.3 billion was authorized by Congress for the Colorado River Water Development Program, to be carried on over a number of years. In Montana for 1969 alone, $61 million was appropriated for work on Libby Dam. All the rivers in the Southwest are being utilized. On the Colorado River is Hoover Dam, which backs up Lake Meade for 117 miles and is capable of storing nearly 30 million acre-feet of water, and in addition furnishes power to a widely divergent area including Arizona and Nevada. Glen Canyon, also on the Colorado, backs up Lake Powell for 186 miles, a dizzying height of concrete that makes the tourist, peering from the parapet, wonder at the temerity of pygmy man who dared to construct such an edifice in the wilderness. Then there is Flaming Gorge on the Green River in Utah, Hell's Canyon on the Snake in Idaho, Yellowtail on the Big Horn in Montana, and the Colorado-Big Thompson project, which consists of a 13-mile water tunnel, five power plants, reservoirs, and irrigation canals for more than 720,000 acres. All over the West such projects have been constructed by the Bureau of Reclamation and the army engineers. In Arizona Senator Carl Hayden said that a project that affected his area ". . . literally means life and continued prosperity to my state."

Ground water has been utilized, too, but so much has been pumped out that restrictions have become necessary to conserve rapidly declining ground-water levels. This is particularly true in Arizona.

Still, there is not sufficient water for predicted population growth in the Southwest, and there is talk of diverting water from states such as Montana and Idaho in the Columbia River Basin to the Southwest and California.

The power and irrigation projects have boosted the local economies during construction, and will in the future; however, they will not have the impact that construction did in the early days, for jobs that were done by men are now done by giant earth-moving machines, diesel tractors, and computers. In the nineteenth century when the railroads were built west, they hired thousands of men and horses and bought tons of feed and lumber. Whole towns erupted overnight.

The billions of federal funds poured into the West are retribution for the vast amounts of land owned by the state and federal governments that, as such, are taken off the tax rolls. This land includes national parks, national forests, Indian reservations and Bureau of Land Management land. In Arizona 84.4 percent of the land is either owned by the state, local, or federal government or is held in trust by the federal government. In Montana 41.3 percent of the land falls in that category; in Colorado, 42 percent; in Idaho, 71 percent; in Utah, 75 percent; in Wyoming, 57 percent; and in New Mexico, 57.9 percent.

The twentieth century has seen a growing expenditure of federal funds in the West. In 1939 the eight Rocky Mountain states received more in subsidies from the government than they paid in taxes. This was also true in 1966. The money, however, cannot be defined as dole; for only the federal government has the funds to develop irrigation and water projects, interstate highways, and national parks. Defense installations might also be included.

Fundamentally, the West has remained a resource area whose wealth has been exaggerated by myth. Thus it was believed that the forests, metals, cattle, and land beyond the Missouri were responsible for the emergence of the United States into a world power. This was overestimating the role these resources played in the national economy. Westerners were particularly prone to boasting of resources and to disparaging manufacturing, which was understandable because there was so little manufacturing in the West. On my first trip east years ago, I watched with wonder as the train slid past the industrial suburbs of a city where grimy brick walls were lettered Goodyear Tire and Rubber Company, Columbia Paints, Mattress Company, Textiles. This was where the things that I used every day were made. Somehow, I had never thought of how or where they were fabricated, but had accepted them as immaculately conceived artifacts.

"The greatest gains in output," one is told by modern economists, "were obtained not from increased quantities of materials but from the reorganization of production functions along capital-intensive lines—that is, by industrialization....

"Thus it was the extension of industrial technique and organization, not only to manufacture and distribution, but to agriculture, mining and forestry as well, that made Western resources economically significant at this point in the nation's history."

The migration of vital, productive people and the pouring of capital into the West were additional factors in the development of its resources.

Before the Civil War the Rocky Mountain West, like the country as a whole, existed in what might be called a colonial-mercantile society, and the world economy was dominated by European powers. During the phenomenal growth period following the Civil War, giant corporations developed steel, transportation, railroads, banking, shipping, and manufacturing of all kinds. The Rocky Mountain West, at first, contributed little to the economic expansion. Iron ore and copper came from Michigan, lumber from Wisconsin and Michigan, and coal from Illinois. By 1900 the economy of the United States had been converted from semi-sufficient sectionalism to national specialization, and resources and manufacturing were directed to country-wide markets.

During the first fifty years of this century, our continued growth was well-nigh unbelievable. Our population doubled, output per capita increased two and one-half times, real national output increased five times, and real personal income per capita rose more than 150 percent.

Before 1910 the contribution of the Rocky Mountain West to this economic growth was almost entirely natural resources. Even then it was not deemed profitable to mine copper ore until after the development of electricity had brought a demand for copper wire. The law of supply and demand, plus the accessibility of the resource due to railroad construction, affected other resources. Demand, also, grew as resources were depleted in other areas.

A popular misconception is that the Rocky Mountain region is the center of the livestock industry. Actually, the West is outranked by Kansas, Nebraska, and Iowa in livestock receipts. But hope is held out for the rancher by the establishment of feed lots and packing plants in the Rocky Mountain region that will cut out the terminal expense and reduce costs through shorter hauls. We saw one such feed lot in eastern New Mexico where 35,000 head were supposedly gaining two and one-half pounds a day on locally purchased milo and imported pellets for the speculators at the feed lot. I didn't ask about antibiotics, although the cattle didn't look too healthy in the belly-deep mud. Since the lot had been in operation for three years, it must have been profitable. Greeley, Colorado, has one of the largest feed lots in the West; the Montana State Planning Board in 1969 had a plan for turning abandoned Glasgow Air Base into a meat processing center with jumbo jets delivering frozen Montana beef to London, Paris, and Tokyo. The only danger to this operation was that the beef might freeze before being processed, since the winter temperatures in Glasgow sometimes drop to forty below zero. Also, any feed lot in the West would have to compete with the midwestern farmer who raises his own luxuriant crops of corn in a humid climate, and thus finds it easy to fatten western range cattle.

As for mining, the future is encouraging in certain respects. With a predicted United States population explosion to 300 million by the year 2000, there will be a great need for metals. Silver in 1969 was expected to soar from $2.50 an ounce to $10 an ounce in ten years time. New copper deposits were being developed in Arizona and Montana, and the chief geologist for the American Smelting and Refining Company reported that new mines were being opened in the Coeur d'Alene district in northern Idaho, which in eighty years had produced 4 billion dollars' worth (in present value) of silver, lead, zinc, copper, and gold.

Add to this, immense reserves of oil, natural gas, coal, and nonferrous metals found in the various western states. Mineral fuels, such as coal, gas, and oil dominate the picture of mineral resources in the West today, and economists see no reason to feel that they will not continue to do so in the future. Leasing, drilling, and the production of petroleum products rose in 1968 to the highest figure in decades, followed by a rise in employment in industry, particularly in Colorado, Wyoming, and New Mexico. But even in Montana the rise has been appreciable. Petroleum production began in Montana in 1915, and by 1960 the state was producing more than 30 million barrels of crude oil annually. In Wyoming, famous for one of the earliest western fields at Teapot Dome, pipelines carry crude oil to local refineries as well as to Salt Lake City and Denver. If one is driving up the north-south highway through Casper, the smell of oil is on the dry, western air, and the round, silver globes of refineries glisten in the sunlight. Oil deposits in Utah, Colorado, and New Mexico that were too deep for exploitation a few decades ago can be made to yield black gold by improved methods of technology. Indeed, geologists have determined that oil and natural gas deposits lie beneath the surface in southeastern Montana, in nearly all of Wyoming, in southern to northeastern Arizona, and in northwestern New Mexico.

This does not mean there are no risks. The government could dump its one million tons of lead and zinc on the market, which would depress the price, or a "technological breakthrough" might eliminate silver as an industrial commodity, or restrictions could be eased on oil imports.

Most important of all, metals, like timber, are exhaustible resources that are being voraciously consumed by our technological society. Despite newer methods of extraction, the time will come when the metals will no longer be there to mine. This shortage is already occurring in timber. A number of large companies like St. Regis, Anaconda, and Potlatch, own their own timber; but many lumber companies depend on national forests where cutting is beyond the sustained yield—that is, where trees are cut faster than they are replaced. Supplies of saw timber in the northern Rocky Mountain region that were abundant in the 1950s are diminishing rapidly.

The only western resource that remains in plentiful supply is land, which is a renewable resource, but again, there are problems. Not only have vast areas been overgrazed and abused, but prices have doubled and tripled in the affluent 1960s. The growth in population and continued inflation have made western land attractive to speculators who buy ranches, subdivide them, and resell them at auction. Entrepreneurs from California and Texas are active in this sort of promotional real estate. Recently, a firm from Atlanta, Georgia, bought an old, established ranch in western Montana, cut it into small parcels, and immediately sold it. The ranchers say that all that keeps them in business is the value of their land, which enables them to borrow at the bank. But it can be a handicap, too; for if a rancher wants to expand, he cannot afford to buy land that is priced as a homesite for Texas or California customers and not for what it will produce.

Another thing that disturbs the economists, but not the state planning boards or the chambers of commerce, who prefer not to think about it, is the dependency of the Rocky Mountain region on the federal government. The growth of manufacturing and the affluence of cities like Colorado Springs, Tucson, and Albuquerque, indeed, the prosperity of all the western states, particularly those in the Southwest, can be attributed to defense plants and defense installations. Even the majority of private industries were attracted by the expenditure of federal funds in this area. The tourist can see the visible signs of wealth for himself: the glass and concrete of the post-World War II buildings, the concrete highways unrolling across the desert, air-conditioned motels with swimming pools. He can also see rows of silver-winged jets behind chain-linked wire and vast stretches where signs say, U.S. Government, No Trespassing.

New Mexico is particularly vulnerable. The state has sixteen major research centers; during 1965-1966 the federal government expenditure in New Mexico exceeded $1 billion, which would be about a thousand dollars per inhabitant. Los Alamos Scientific Laboratory (the place where the atomic bomb was assembled) is near Santa Fe in the piñon-pine foothills. The White Sands Missile Range, the Sandia Laboratories in Albuquerque (which hold a prime contract with the Atomic Energy Commission), the USAF Special Weapons Center at Kirkland Air Base in Albuquerque, and the USAF Missile Development Center at Holloman Air Base are all in New Mexico. The list could continue for pages. In Arizona Fort Huachuca, which is the Army's electronic proving ground, spurred the growth of manufacturing of transistors, computers, and electronics in Tucson and the surrounding area. Aircraft and aircraft components are also manufactured in Arizona, and Motorola is the largest industrial employer in the state. The plants that manufacture these products are greatly sought after because the products are in the high-value, low-weight classification, which lessens transportation costs.

In 1969 when appropriations for the aerospace industry and the antiballistic missile system were in doubt, cutbacks in employment threatened New Mexico. In Montana a proposed 75 percent decrease in federal aid to the states for construction, including highway projects, was termed by the Governor as "almost disastrous."

Montana is one of the states, among others in the Rocky Mountain region, that has a high proportion of very young people under twenty-one and very old people, sixty-five and over in comparison with workers of productive age. What this means is that when young men and women receive an education, they leave the state to seek jobs elsewhere, because there are few employment opportunities in their home areas. This so-called youth drain is of serious concern to state officials because it puts an undue burden on the few active workers who remain. Perhaps, more than anything else, this explodes the myth of opportunity in the West.

Big government and big corporations control the land. There are few individuals left, such as the Montana rancher who last autumn wrote to Tiffany's requesting a diamond ring that would not cost more than $200 "because that's all I sold my cow for."

Conservation --
The Cry in the Wilderness

VIII

The representative of the Industrial Division from the Department of Development for the State of New Mexico was a personable young man—convincing and dedicated. The young man's office was not as large nor his staff as extensive as his counterparts' offices in Utah, Salt Lake City, or Colorado. The Rocky Mountain states see the need for industrial development boards, but not all can afford the public relations, advertising, and salesmanship necessary to attract industry.

"Yes," the young man said, "we're hoping to get a pulp mill south of here."

"Are you being opposed by conservationists?"

"Oh yes, that's to be expected, but people needn't

121

worry. I inspected a number of mills in Canada that had no noxious odors or smoke, and our mill will have the same modern equipment."

"People in western Montana were assured there'd be no smoke from a pulp mill that was built there, and they've been fighting it ever since."

The young man was unperturbed, "I understand there's been trouble with that mill—a Kraft sulphate process, I think."

He did not feel that it was necessary to add that if it were not for the pulp mill, the local sawmills and lumber operations could only operate sporadically, and the community would lose jobs that it could ill afford to lose.

A year later, my husband and I sat next to another young man at a meeting of the Environmental Council at the University of Montana. The young man was from Albuquerque and had moved to Montana because Albuquerque had grown too large. He said to us, "You have the same problems concerning the environment up here that we have in New Mexico, except that we were lucky—we stopped the construction of a pulp mill they tried to build south of Santa Fe."

The room where the meeting was held was so crowded that people had to stand. The majority were men over thirty and they represented—along with the women—a varied segment of the population: housewives, faculty, TV and newspaper reporters, retired citizens, a state legislator, packers, dude ranchers, representatives of the League of Women Voters, the Garden Clubs, and the Association of University Women, an Indian, officials of the Fish and Game Commission, the Wilderness Society, the Wildlife Federation, and half a dozen students. Such a group would have been difficult to find ten years ago in the West; today many similar groups are active in communities.

The older members welcomed the students, and the

chairman asked if the boys had anything to say. A youth wearing long hair and metal-rimmed glasses stood up. "There aren't many of us interested in this environment thing yet— only about 30 out of the 8,000 in the school—but we think we've made ourselves heard in the state capital and we're going to attend meetings on the wilderness areas."

The student was articulate and well informed; his numbers would grow—the biggest encouragement to conservation in a long time.

A packer—to whom preservation of the environment was a serious project because his livelihood depended on it— got to his feet to request support from the Forest Service against pressure from the Woods Products Industry. He was willing to go back to Washington, if need be. "I may not be good, but I'm loud!"

The grey-haired main speaker was a recognized authority on the environment. His subject was a report by a federal commission on public lands. "Tremendous pressures are being exerted by industry. If we want to counteract those pressures, we must write letters—write to our representatives in Washington to let them know we want the quality of the environment preserved."

Additional subjects on the program were pesticides, the Forest Service practice of allowing clear-cut logging, and the establishment of wilderness areas, which was being held up in a congressional committee. In the East and in heavily populated areas, environmental problems—such as what to do about smog from automobile exhaust in Los Angeles or how to dispose of sewage in Chicago—are caused by too many people and the concentration of industry. In the West the problems are caused mainly by the pressure of industry (in the guise of out-of-state corporations). Interested in such natural resources as lumber and mining, these corporations ex-

ploit the wilderness areas. Major problems are also caused by
the Corps of Engineers—pressured by power companies—to
construct dams.

To the audience the projects were more than names.
They had seen the mountainsides mutilated like a battlefield
by clear-cut logging that left zigzag scars of roads, rocks, and
charred stumps, where once there had been a national forest;
they had walked by streams where the water a few years ago
had been sweet and cool to drink but now was contaminated
by D.D.T. and green with algae; they had inspected the so-
called recreational lakes created by dams during the draw-
down that exposed mud flats snagged by stumps.

In other Rocky Mountain states people were banding
together to protest a mining company bulldozing roads into
the White Cloud Mountains of Idaho; they were fighting
against construction of the High Mountain Sheep Dam on the
Snake River for power interests; they were trying to preserve
desert areas—abloom in spring with yellow poppies and
cream and scarlet cactus—from the real estate developers.

These projects entail considerable cost and discouragement to industry in a region that, according to the economists, needs manufacturing to raise a low per capita income.
The Rocky Mountain states are a resource area; that is, the attractions for industry are based on the exploitation of its natural resources. And most of these resources are located on public lands administered by the Forest Service and the Bureau
of Public Lands for the American people.

The conservationists, according to an economics professor at the University of Montana, are "those who have the
least to lose economically"; that is, the middle-income group,
salaried employees (largely of governmental or semiprivate,
nonindustrial concerns), and professional people.

Conservationists have also been identified by those who

hold opposing views as "nature fakers," "pinkos" (especially if they are college professors with beards), and "crackpots against progress," which is the worst sin of all.

Industrialists and some businessmen and federal employees oppose the conservationists. Allied with the former group, according to the economics professor, are "the low wage earner, the marginal worker, the already poor."

A government commitment to defeat pollution, the professor said, would lower the American standard of living, because if any society is to survive, it must produce the goods and services that are required for its own perpetuation. Payment for a higher quality environment could mean higher prices for cardboard boxes, lumber, trout fishing, recreational use of public lands, and automobiles.

Woods workers and miners are particularly concerned. At the check-out stand of a supermarket, I heard a fellow in jeans and a hard hat cursing a recent demonstration of Girls Against Smog and Pollution. "They'd think different if they got their pay check from the mill."

Conservationists identify these people and others who sympathize with them as "shortsighted," "company men," and "John Birchers."

Between the battle lines stand the politicians and the federal employees who decide the policy on public lands and who do not like to commit themselves one way or another on such a controversial subject as conservation. These people are supposed to represent the public, but according to Donald Jackson in an article in *Life* in January of 1970, "Nobody who speaks for the public seems willing, or able, to exercise control." This was in particular reference to the White Cloud Mountain debate, but it could apply to numerous other instances. However, in justice to the federal employees and to our political representatives, it should be said that the majority, considering the lobbying to which they are subjected, are doing the best job they can.

Whatever "side" the individual is on, the conservationists and anti-conservationists agree that the quality of the environment will be an explosive issue in the coming decades due to our rapidly expanding population and technology. For the first time in the evolution of man, we are faced with the prospect of too many people on earth. Dr. John Knowles, director of the Massachusetts General Hospital, said that we have already exceeded the optimum population from the public-health point of view. It took 1600 years to double the world population of 250 million; today the more than 3 billion people on earth will double in 35 years. Add to that a predicted increase in the economy of $1 trillion dollars a year and fantastic advances in technology that demand an increased use of metals, nonferrous minerals, power, water, lumber, and space. The pressure on the land and its remaining resources will grow greater year by year. While the problem is nationwide, it is particularly pertinent in the Rocky Mountain West where space still survives; where Americans can claim the few existing wilderness areas, the last wild rivers, and game species, such as the grizzly bear and the coyote.

The more intangible values, scoffed at by the anti-conservationists, are not as easy to define. Perhaps the best way to explain these would be to say that man occasionally needs to be alone, with only the sounds of water and wind in the trees and a glimpse of stars above the mountains. In the wilderness he assumes his proper perspective with the universe. There he can find his personal God, courage and peace from the earth that sustains him in life and to which he will return in death. Did not Christ, in his agony, go into the Garden? A doctor who heads one of the most famous mental clinics in the nation emphasizes the value of the wilderness for relieving the tensions that beset modern man.

The westerner sees these wilderness areas being despoiled by industry and knows that once they are gone, they will be gone forever. In his fight to preserve them, he is handicapped by the myth of inexhaustible resources. In the *American Commonwealth* in 1887, James Bryce wrote, "These people are intoxicated with the majestic scale of the nature in which their lot is cast, enormous mineral deposits, boundless prairies, forests which, even squandered—wickedly squandered—as they are now, will supply timber for the United States for centuries."

Lord Bryce overestimated the timber supply and underestimated industry. Otherwise, he was right about the American illusion of wealth bestowed by nature. Since the first trappers blustered into the wilderness, Americans have exploited natural resources without regard to their limitation. Indeed, the American ethic is founded on the growth of industry and population, and nowhere has this been accepted with greater faith than in the Rocky Mountain West.

In the journals of the fur traders, there was—as far as I have read—no concern about the unrestrained trapping of fur-bearing animals. Charles Larpenteur of the American Fur Company in 1835 listed with satisfaction that a trader in one season brought in 9,000 buffalo robes, 1,020 beaver, and 2,800 muskrat. White wolves, swanskins, and bear hides also found a market. Whatever was profitable was baled and sold to American or European merchants.

After the trappers came the buffalo hunters, who in less than a decade slaughtered the immense herds that once grazed from Canada to the Rio Grande. Tourists on trains amused themselves by shooting at the animals near the tracks. The hunters took only the tongues and the hides, leaving the carcasses to putrefy on the prairie. The tongues were considered a delicacy, and the hides brought $3 apiece. Only a few people and the Indians, whose livelihood was being destroyed, were sickened by the butchery. In a few short years between 1874 and 1879, General Nelson A. Miles estimated that five million buffalo were killed.

There were also bounty hunters who poisoned the wolves and the coyotes, who had kept the ecological balance by living off the weaker calves and the old buffalo. Once I saw a coyote who had been poisoned; in his agony he ran in circles, chewing at his belly before he went into convulsions. He died in a short while. Sometimes, if they get only a small amount of poison, it takes them longer to die—several days or even a week.

There are still bounties on predators in most western states, and people with dogs are cautioned not to let them get coyote bait. The cattlemen and sheepmen insist on the bounties because they claim that coyotes and mountain lions kill lambs and calves, which are valuable on the present-day market. Some conservationists dispute this, saying that ranchers exaggerate the number of calves and lambs killed. They point to an increase in field mice, gophers, and other small, harmful rodents with the disappearance of the predators.

Sportsmen have killed without thought to the future, too. Indeed, sportsmen and sporting-goods companies have been among the leading proponents of the myth of boundless game herds. In the West hunting is a prerogative of the American male, whose ego is boosted by donning a red shirt and hat, climbing into a jeep, and driving up a logging road until he sees a deer. Sometimes he makes what is called a "sound shot," that is, he shoots at a sound in the bushes without seeing what caused it and kills another hunter. Such accidents are growing in number every hunting season as the game decreases.

In the past wealthy eastern and European sportsmen, such as Lord Dunraven, whose "kill" ran into the thousands, journeyed to the Rocky Mountains. Venison and elk meat were standard fare in the mining and cow camps. My father told me that when the Milwaukee Railroad was being built through Montana, the crew-cooks would toss a stick of dynamite into the river for enough fish to feed a hundred or more men.

This callous disregard for wild life has had the inevitable result. Ten or fifteen years ago I could walk in the forest and see a doe watching me with upflung head or hear the slap of a beaver's tail as he dove beneath the water. There would be tracks in the wet sand of the creeks, and all around I could feel life and movement. Now the woods are like an empty house, and there are even fewer birds than before.

I grew up believing in the western myth. I hunted deer, gophers, coyotes, antelope, and ducks. On opening day we expected as a matter of course to get our limit of green-necked mallards and small, blue-winged teal. Even in the mid-1960s I stood on a hill in the dawn mist and heard the rush of countless wings and the crying of wild geese. Three years later I waited on the same hill, as the stars faded and the sky paled behind the mountains, so that I could see the reeds reflected in the waters of the pond and hear to the north the guns of the hunters signaling the legal shooting time. From the north, seeking safety from the hunters, came a flight of wild geese, not the countless hundreds that I had seen before, but only a "V" of half a dozen, crying like lost children. They came in low, so low that I could not miss, even with a sixteen-gauge shotgun. A goose plummeted to the ground, and I ran forward to the ditch where it had fallen. It lay in the mud, its head doubled beneath folded wings, and I looked at it and then sat down on the bank and wept.

Land has been exploited like the game. The cattlemen and the sheepmen overstocked the range, destroying the grass, so that in its place have sprouted knapweed, thistles, sagebrush, and many other noxious plants. The homesteaders plowed submarginal acreage, and the wind blew away the topsoil. Gold miners dredged the streams, leaving heaps of gravel for miles in the once fertile valleys. Poisonous emissions from smelters shriveled the vegetation, leaving a desolation of barren hills. Look at the Coeur d'Alene district of northern Idaho where the valley is heaped with black slag or Anaconda, Montana—location of another smelter—where nothing has grown on the hills for more than half a century.

Still in effect is the mining law of 1872 that permits exploration by mining companies in wilderness areas, which means that roads can be bulldozed into fragile, scenic areas; drilling and even open-pit mining can result. The pressure from mining corporations on public lands increases with the increase in technology. The millions of babies born every week will need oil from the shale in Colorado, Wyoming, and Utah that can only be loosened by a nuclear blast. New copper deposits will be needed with the appropriation of mines in foreign countries, and this means water and air pollution. In eastern Montana and Wyoming lie vast coal resources to fuel the power plants for the megalopolis. The coal in Montana is low in sulphur and so would be desirable to burn in midwestern power plants; but transportation rates are high, and the mining companies do not want to add the cost of reclaiming the devastated land to that of production.

The greatest pressures are on the forests that are owned by the states, by private companies or individuals, by railroads who acquired the forests in land grants, and, in particular, by the National Forests. These national forests belong to the American people, but they have been administered, in some instances, for the benefit of lumber firms. In 1965 a record 1,402,188,520 board-feet of timber was harvested in the sixteen national forests of the Northern Region alone. This was still not enough; in 1969 a number of timber-supply bills were introduced into Congress, ostensibly to improve national forest-timber management, but actually to increase the volume of logging. These bills followed a meeting of lumbermen from twelve western states in Portland, Oregon, where the discussion centered around a "mutual understanding" between commercial timber interests and the custodians of public lands. Many of the logging firms represented depended on timber from public lands sold at auction.

Early logging companies cut ties for the railroads, stulls for the mines, and timber for boards for rapidly building towns. When the forests in Michigan and Wisconsin were exhausted, the logging companies moved to the Pacific Coast and then to the untouched forests of the Rockies. Logging is an industry closely associated with the supply of standing timber. In the Southeast and Northeast the lumber industry reports large returns, but this is due to the manufacture of pulp. The West specializes in lumber and lumber products due to the species of timber available and to the national forests that so far have been protected from over-cutting.

My father was one of the midwestern lumbermen who moved to Montana in the early part of the twentieth century. He said that when he arrived, he could travel by train through western Montana and Idaho and see forests for endless miles—white pine and larch and ponderosa. Some of the trees were three and four feet in diameter and three hundred years old. The lumber companies had no difficulty finding trees to cut in those days, and they did so with wanton disregard for the future. Under the Timber and Stone Act large timber tracts were filed by lumberjacks and turned over to the lumber companies who logged them off and then let the land, littered with stumps and dead branches, revert to the government. If fires started from logging operations, they were allowed to burn; or if sparks from the railroad locomotives fell into brush along the tracks, no one bothered to quench the flames. This was how the great fire of 1910 grew from myriad small fires to the great conflagration that "crowned" all the way from the Canadian border to Colorado. The general attitude was that the more trees cut, the greater the progress. Only a few persons were disturbed by the logging, and it was not until the administration of Theodore Roosevelt, who was advised by Gifford Pinchot, that a real effort was made to establish a Forest Service and national forests.

As wasteful as the lumber companies were in the early days, they could only do a limited amount of damage because they relied on manpower, not mechanical equipment. The lumberjacks felled the trees with crosscut saws—one man on each end of the saw—and the logs were snaked out by teams. Logging was a personal operation, and there was a close relationship between the woods and the lumberjacks who were a lusty, independent lot in their stagged pants, cleated boots, and small-brimmed hats. All my life I shall remember one broad-shouldered fellow in a checked shirt trying to break a logjam in the river during the spring flood. Cant hook in hand, he lept the jackstrawed heap of logs to find the key log so that he could wrench it free and start the drive again. One misstep and he would have been swept into the roar of water; he dared the river, exultant in his skill.

Logging today is a far different operation, more efficient and impersonal. Lumberjacks are better paid and better educated; they use chain saws to cut the trees, bulldozers to push the roads into areas too high and remote to log before, and mechanical means to load the logs onto trucks. The modern woods worker isn't even called a lumberjack, he is a skilled mechanic in a hard hat driving a "cat" or a truck or operating a chain saw. He has little feeling for the forest because he drives to the end of the road in his own car; when he quits at night, he drives home to his family who usually lives in a mobile home.

Some farsighted lumber companies, such as the St. Regis Paper Company in northwestern Montana, use selective logging methods; that is, a few trees are left to shelter the young growth, and an attempt is made to preserve the fragile soil. These companies are looking to the future and managing their forests as the Europeans have for generations on a commercial, practical basis. The Forest Service insists that they are doing the same thing, but by allowing clear-cutting and—so some experts say—cutting beyond the sustained yield, they have aroused a great deal of criticism. Indeed, the image of the handsome young Ranger in his hard-brimmed hat accompanied by Smokey the Bear has become somewhat tarnished. Clear-cutting leaves nothing standing. The area is then burned, and sometimes the devastated mountainsides are mechanically terraced. Critics say clear-cutting results in erosion and destruction of the watershed. Doubts are also expressed about the effectiveness of reforestation—a few inches high seedling planted in a dry, crumbly earth where, before the delicate ecosystem was disturbed, it took from 100 to 150 years for a pine to mature in the semiarid region.

In defense, the Forest Service brings in experts to testify to the advantages of "harvesting" the "overmature" timber in this fashion. There are swarms of experts; for the Forest Service has grown into a very large government department. The experts are capable, and most of them are sincere; but conservationists feel there are too many personnel in the harvesting of resources and not enough in the protection of the watersheds, wildlife, and soils. Lumbermen, for their part, are more blunt; they say lumber is needed for housing and pulp for containers and paper. They point to a study made by the Western Woods Products Association in which it was estimated that the 1969 housing starts in the West would grow from 150,000 units annually to about 550,000 units annually in the period from 1971 to 1975. This, the lumbermen emphasize, is in the West only. Sixty percent of the timber would have to come from national forests, and a Woods Products Association official declared that production is seriously threatened by what he called a current wave of emotional concern.

The lumbermen are supported by many businessmen and state politicians; a percentage from the timber sales goes to counties for schools and roads, a percentage that can add up to a sizable sum for a poor county where the tax base is limited by large tracts of federally-owned land.

The one subject that lumbermen do not like to discuss is wood substitutes. European houses are not built of wood, why should houses in America continue to be built of wood? Modern architects are becoming interested in the potentials of concrete. The production of paper and cardboard containers could be curtailed without damaging the economy.

The lumber companies have powerful lobbies, as do the oil and mining interests; the government departments are also influential in Washington. The conservationists cannot compete with them financially, although the Sierra Club is becoming more and more a force to be reckoned with, as is the Wilderness Society. Conservationists still depend to a great extent on individuals, like the zoology professor from the University of Montana who, severely limited by funds, flew back to Washington to testify for the Lincoln Back-

Country Wilderness—a fragile, unspoiled area the professor had worked hard to preserve from what the Forest Service terms "multiple use." Lumber representatives also testified and a number of impartial citizens were asked to give their views. One individual from Montana stood up to say how he felt the Lincoln Back-Country would benefit from logging. At the end of his speech, he said, "I would also like to give thanks for my all-expenses-paid trip back here . . .," naming a representative of a lumber company.

Conservationists cannot afford to subsidize witnesses. Indeed, money severely limits their activities. They suffer from other handicaps too. They tend to equate conservation, which should be bipartisan, with political and social issues. They interest themselves in local problems and fail to cooperate on the problems of other areas, and they tend to gather in vociferous groups, ignoring people they do not know. On occasion they become prejudiced and emotional, frightening the silent majority who do not want to become too deeply involved, but who are beginning to be concerned and whose support is necessary to achieve results. These are the people who work on noncontroversial projects such as the Red Cross, the church, and community fund drives. Total commitment on conservation can lead to hostility from segments of the community and financial retaliation to the businessman.

However, intelligent industrialists realize they must cooperate to preserve the environment, even though it adds to costs. Another encouraging note is the involvement of the government, politicians, and students in conservation.

It could be that population growth and exploitation of natural resources no longer mean expansion. Our resources are near depletion, and one has only to look at India and China to realize that large populations do not mean prosperity. As a student in an environmental seminar said, "I question the need for economic expansion at too great cost."

In the final analysis, what happens to the few remaining unspoiled regions of the West depends on the American people who own them.

Shake Hands, Boys--
Politics in the Open Spaces

IX

The candidate for sheriff wore high-heeled boots and a big hat; his weight threatened to collapse the chair on which he sat, before the American flag. He didn't make much of a speech, but that didn't matter; the entertainment was the main attraction, a tall, skinny fellow singing and plucking a guitar:

> Oh, my pretty Quadroon,
> My flower that faded too soon . . .

Everyone in the audience knew the candidate, and his election was assured. His opponent was a newcomer to the county and didn't have a chance.

This was the way elections should be, I thought—

137

government of the people, by the people, and for the people. Not until years later did I realize how I, tike so many others, had been deceived by the western myth.

The election of the sheriff had been assured, not because he was the best man for the job and not because the people wanted him, but because he had been backed by the mining monopoly, the Cattlemen's Association, and the railroads.

Government in the West, as well as other parts of the United States, was, and still is, subject to pressure groups. Indeed, for a period in the past, it was disgracefully dominated by special interests and characterized by corruption and violence.

Increasing urbanization might be expected to have a liberalizing influence on state governments; but so far, this has not been the case, and political pollsters who identify urbanization with liberalization tear their hair and call the West unpredictable.

The West in a period of transition has problems not shared by other parts of the country, and these problems do not attract the attention in Washington that the problems of the more heavily populated areas do. The reason is plain to see; all eight states have only nineteen Congressmen (Arizona and Colorado gained one more apiece in the 1970 census), which is less than half the representation of California or New York. In addition, all eight states have fewer than forty electoral votes, while New York had forty-three in the 1968 election and California had forty. Population gains in the 1970s, the pollsters predict, will not make an appreciable difference.

The West, says Dr. Frank Jonas of the Political Science Department of the University of Utah, does not have the vote to determine its own destiny, which is largely decided by the federal government and out-of-state corporations, although this could be modified by the influx in the last few years of politically conscious people and the increasing interest in politics of the young.

Westerners who listen to returns in general elections are accustomed to commentators who excitedly quote the votes from what they call the "key" states and who say, "Oh, yes, we have the final returns from Nevada (three electoral votes), but first let's see what's happening in California."

In the last election I thought the commentators had completely forgotten Nevada, and they did neglect to report Montana until the final returns had been in for half an hour from that state.

Politics, like the economy, result from a great land area, sparsely populated and semiarid, a region of natural resources where more than 50 percent of the land is government owned. Government monies account for a disproportionate expenditure of funds. This does not exclude Colorado and Arizona that are classified as the most economically progressive of the Rocky Mountain states.

The sparseness of the population accounts for its political unpredictability; for candidates are frequently elected on an individual, rather than a party basis. The pollsters should also take into account the westerners' enthusiasm for participating in government. In the late 1850s, Albert Richardson wrote:

"Making governments and building towns are the natural employments of the migratory Yankee. He takes to them as instinctively as a young duck to water. Congregate a hundred Americans anywhere beyond the settlements, and they immediately lay out a city, frame a state constitution, and apply for admission into the Union, while twenty-five of them become candidates for the United States Senate."

In heavily populated areas, the electorate does not have the opportunity to personally participate in politics. The candidates are images on television or pictures in the newspa-

140

per. In Montana people call the majority leader of the Senate, Mike Mansfield, by his first name. Mansfield says, "I don't know of any other state where they refer to senators by first names. It indicates a close relationship, which is good."

Mansfield is wrong about Montana's informality not extending to other places; many political representatives are called by their first names in all the Rocky Mountain states.

In New Mexico as well as Montana, in Idaho as well as Utah, attending the legislature when it is in session is a favorite pastime. This personal contact does not mean, however, nor has it meant in the past, a liberal or representative government free of pressure from vested interests. It just means that people know their representatives; those they don't know, they know of and have no compunctions about asking them to intercede in this or that bill in which they are interested. Since air travel is erratic in the Northwest in the winter and limited at the best of times in small communities, a trip to the legislature means driving hundreds of miles, frequently through blizzards, rain, or sandstorms. Women's clubs come en masse; high school classes fill the galleries so students can be introduced to their representatives. If you have a Senator friend, he asks you to "sit on the floor" where you can watch the legislative process close up, which means paying attention to the speakers and not being distracted by pages bringing paper cups of coffee and the lights flashing on the voting panel. Sometimes a legislator will ask you to dinner or lunch, and the discussion will give you a delightful feeling of being on the inside of what's going on. All this is hard on the legislators, but it is great fun for their constituents.

In recent years the population growth of Colorado, Arizona, and, possibly Utah—where politics are colored by the Church of Latter-day Saints—has diluted the personal touch. More legislators are elected from the metropolitan statistical areas where voters are not acquainted with their representatives. At the same time, the voters in the rural areas hesitate to invade the marble halls of a capitol that has grown increasingly sophisticated in its urban setting.

The legislatures of the eight states share certain problems, such as the issues between liberals and conservatives, the financing of schools and other state institutions and services, the administration of state-owned lands, conservation, health and welfare programs, the sales tax and how to increase it, the availability of federal funds, and the question of how to attract industry in order to broaden the tax base. Through all these problems runs the theme of the dependence of the West on other parts of the country.

At a meeting of the Federation of Rocky Mountain States, which has been established to deal with common problems, Jack Campbell, ex-governor of New Mexico, expressed it this way: "We'd like to see a north-south orientation instead of the present east-west emphasis through the Rocky Mountains."

The legislatures have their special problems, too. In Arizona people say that "water is politics." In Montana thousands of acre-feet of water annually flow out of the state, 63 percent into the Columbia and 37 percent through the Missouri Basin. The Southwest—California, too—covets this water, and friction has developed between the arid and less arid parts of the West, and in the future will continue to do so as population increases demand more water than is presently available. In Nevada the scarcity of arable land and water creates a dependency on gambling and tourism, so that the problem is how to tax the casinos without discouraging that lucrative source of revenue. The advent of people of wealth has boosted the economy with a resultant effect on the politics of a state that was already benefiting by its success in at-

tracting industry and the millionaires by no personal or corporate income tax and no inheritance or estate tax.

In Arizona and Colorado many of the problems arise
from the influx of new people attracted by new industry,
which means a greater demand for schools and services of all
kinds; while in New Mexico, the greatest problem is the
undue dependency of the state's economy on the federal government. Utah has a large Mormon population. For years in
the past the hostility between Gentiles and Mormons disrupted Utah politics. Today the Church influences the legislature,
but it does not dominate it. A non-Mormon can win at the
polls if he does not antagonize the Church, which tends toward conservatism, although Mormons vote for both parties.

Legislators are predominately white and middle aged. A
survey of Montana's legislature in 1968 showed that of 159
members, 54 were ranchers and farmers; 29, businessmen;
19, attorneys; 16, professional people; and 8, educators. Seventy-two, or more than two-thirds, were from ranches or
small towns of less than 2,500. Only 21 were from towns of
between 2,500 and 10,000. Two-thirds were college graduates, and the median age in the Senate, which was dominated
by the Democrats, was fifty-three, while the median age in
the House, which was dominated by Republicans, was two
years younger. Six representatives in the House were in their
twenties; none in that age bracket were in the Senate. The
rural representation in the northwestern states is higher than
it is in Colorado, Utah, and Arizona. From personal observation, I noticed more high-heeled boots and big hats in the
lobbies at Helena and Cheyenne than in Denver or Salt Lake
City, which is a disappointment to tourists because the legis-
lator-rancher is a part of the western myth. So are the spit-
toons that used to abound in capitol halls and that have been
removed, occasioning some inconvenience to those gentle-

men who still chew.

Urban representation, it might be explained, does not mean a more liberal legislature, because any town of 2,500 or over is classified as an urban area; there are numbers of such towns in the West, while there are only four cities of 100,000 or over in the eight states. A town with a population of 2,500 can remain rural in interest if not designation, especially if it borders a wilderness area or several hundred miles of desert. Also, in Arizona where Phoenix tends to vote conservative, the area has witnessed an influx of older people from the Midwest. Adding to the confusion is the weakness in all the states of party affiliations; a Democrat may vote for a conservative measure or a Republican may support the liberals.

In the new legislative building at Sante Fe, which has a speaker's platform draped like a stage, we heard the members of the House arguing about an "obscene and filthy" poem that had been circulated by an instructor in an English class at the University of New Mexico.

"Do you think the best use of tax dollars is for the teaching of 'gutter literature'?" an irate legislator demanded.

"Sounds familiar, doesn't it?" the friend sitting with me in the gallery said, and I agreed. The same argument concerning another piece of pornographic literature was being debated with equal feeling in the capitol of Montana. The only difference was that in Montana the instructor was not dismissed as was the one in New Mexico.

In recent years the conservative has expressed mistrust of the liberal academic community and of student activists, especially those with long hair and beards. The universities are thought to be centers for sin, speed, and socialism. American flag decals decorate cars in rebuttal to peace marches that, in most cases, consist of a dozen students straggling downtown to listen to a speech by a professor before the recruiting office or the local industry that pollutes the environment.

The arrangment works very well. The University serves as a goad to a region that otherwise might stiffen into bigotry while the community acts as a balance to the radical elements who equate emotional immaturity with social justice. Communities and universities combined have worked for legislation on conservation, welfare, and civil improvement. It is too bad that branches of the universities cannot be located in all western communities; for the more remote a town is from a university, the more apt it is to be ultraconservative. Miles City, the cowtown capital on the eastern Montana prairie, is an example of countless similar towns—Vernal, Utah; Salmon, Idaho; Sundance, Wyoming—the list is endless. The inhabitants of Miles City and the ranchers from the surrounding country are hard-working, honest citizens who feel a responsibility to their country. In World War I and II the volunteer enlistments from the West exceeded the national average. Westerners not only worked for their country, they died for it, and today men are disturbed by the social and economic changes that have convulsed the world. Their taxes and expenses are rising rapidly, while livestock prices remain what they were twenty years ago, which results in a mistrust of labor unions, a concern for law and order, and a misunderstanding of racial unrest. Long-time Democrats are turning into Republicans.

A rancher-oil trucker interviewed in 1968 said in reply to a question about race relations, "I don't think the Negro is any different from our Indian. You don't see our Indians rioting. Any Indian or Negro who wants to better himself can do it."

Eastern Montanans are accustomed to Indians, but few of them visit the reservations. In 1968 in Miles City, there was only one Negro, who was a bootblack.

Distrust of the federal government, influenced by cities and big business in the East, is deep rooted in the West. In the early days when the emigrants crossed the Missouri, they envisioned a West that would evolve its own political as well as economic destiny, although even the land in which they settled was admitted to the Union more for the convenience of eastern interests than western desires. Arizona, when it became a state in 1912, did so with a progressive constitution that included provision for a recall process; Wyoming was the first state to extend woman suffrage, and Montana elected the first Congresswoman. Labor battled for reforms in the mountains as it did in the Pennsylvanian coal fields in the 1880s and 1890s, and as a result, labor has exerted considerable influence in the Colorado and Montana legislatures.

In the last decades of the nineteenth century and in the first of the twentieth, the West was considered politically liberal, even socialistic. This was a time, it must be remembered, when the laboring man received little consideration in court, and society, in general, favored capital. The popular opinion among businessmen was that expressed by a banker and railroad man who lived next door to us when I was a child. I remember him as a pompous gentleman with a heavy mustache and a gold chain draped across his stomach. During construction of the Milwaukee railroad sometime before I was born, Mr. Lusk declared, "All construction cost is based upon the cost of labor that does the work, and any saving in cost generally means more railroads and more consequent development."

To minimize costs (and increase railroad profits for the Milwaukee that was backed by Standard Oil), Italians and Montenegrins were imported to do unskilled labor by labor contractors who received so much a head. The daily wage, which was about that of the lumberjacks and hard-rock miners, averaged $2.50 for an eight- to ten-hour shift. Board of seventy-five cents a day came out of this and twenty cents per day for the first five days for thirty days of medical treatment. After the thirty days the man, if he was still ill or crippled, became a county charge. Men could be fired without notice, and wages were cut during hard times, such as the panic of 1893 and that of 1907. The Italians were known as "Wops" and the Montenegrins as "Mountain Niggers"; when a Montenegrin leader was shot by a white hoodlum, the white man was turned loose with the comment by a local law officer that the Montengrin was only "an ignorant nigger, anyhow."

Simultaneously, the farmers and small ranchers were finding that the agrarian utopia was, indeed, a myth and that the cheap colonist rates advertised by the railroads to lure them to settlement on submarginal land had lured them to disaster. All over the West anger smouldered and began to burn in the hearts of the men whose shoulders stooped beneath the crossed straps of their overalls and in the hearts of their women who were old before their time from child bearing and hard labor, but mostly from despair. The anger spread to the hard-rock miners in Cripple Creek who could not feed their children and to the lumberjacks who had only the poorhouse to look forward to if they were injured in their perilous work. When the Sherman Silver Purchase Act was repealed in 1893, sending the price of silver still lower and resulting in more jobs lost to miners, people felt the government had cheated the West. They did not see that silver was in oversupply and that the price was bound to decline anyhow or that the farmers had not been forced, but had chosen to take up homesteads on submarginal land. They saw only the booming prosperity of industry, and they blamed the "money trusts" and the railroads. Thus, a so-called "agrarian revolt" erupted in the Midwest and spread to the Rocky Mountains when the farmers included a free silver plank in the platform of what became known as the Populist Party, which advocated free coinage of silver, a graduated income tax and public ownership of the railroads.

Corporate business reacted with alarm, and when violence broke out in the mines in Colorado, Montana, and Idaho, the Populists were called fanatics and dangerous radicals. In 1893 the Western Federation of Miners was organized in Butte, Montana, and strikes spread to Cripple Creek, Leadville, and Telluride in Colorado. The mine owners went to court and secured injunctions against the union in order to allow the operation of the mines by "scab" labor, whereupon the miners retaliated by dynamiting the mines and beating up the scabs. Encouraged by the success of the miners, labor organizers appeared in the lumber camps. The Populists elected a governor of Colorado and in 1896 allied with the Democrats to back a westerner, William Jennings Bryan, as presidential nominee. At the convention Bryan made his famous speech:

". . . Burn down your cities and leave our farms, and your cities will spring up again as if by magic; but destroy our farms and the grass will grow in the streets of every city in our country.

"Having behind us the producing masses of this nation and the world, . . . the labor interests, and the toilers everywhere, we will answer . . . by saying . . . . You shall not press down upon the brow of labor this crown of thorns, you shall not crucify mankind upon a cross of gold."

What words to inspire the hard-rock miner, the lumberjack, and the homesteader! But the West lost its bid for political power, even though Bryan took the electoral votes of every state west of the Mississippi except five. And so the West suffered defeat and, many felt, another and final betrayal.

Violence continued in the mines and the lumber camps and the homesteaders expressed temporary but futile dissatisfaction at the polls; the West never again gained sufficient power to influence the national scene. La Follette and President Theodore Roosevelt broke the power of the big-money trusts, and the I.W.W. (Industrial Workers of the World) forced labor reforms. This did not stop the decline in mining, drought on the prairies, or rising prices for manufactured goods. During World War I the farmers responded by growing crops and raising cattle to feed the nation; when the war was over, agricultural prices fell. The East, after a temporary recession, boomed during the twenties, but in the West banks closed, homesteads were sold at auction, and mines were abandoned. Long before the thirties, the West knew the bitterness of failure.

The ranchers in Salmon, Idaho, in Utah, in Arizona and Miles City remember this, and so do many people in the small towns. If their experience was not personal, they heard what happened from their fathers, and so during the 1960s they opposed reapportionment, because they thought it would increase the political power of the urban areas, and they reacted fiercely to a gun control law, which they considered an infringement on personal liberties. In the West men have always carried guns for hunting, to kill predators, and for protection. If you drive along a Western highway, you can't help noticing the gun racks in the back windows of pick-up trucks. The gun control law, westerners felt, discriminated against the West in an attempt to control crime in the big cities.

The newcomers and the younger people are not so independent. Nurtured in an affluent society, they do not remember the blowing dust and the bread lines. They have come to accept dependency on the government as a matter of course and to recognize what the older native-born westerner will not—that the West has always depended on the government to regulate railroads, build reclamation projects, stockpile metals, construct highways, administer the public lands, and, since World War II, boost the economy by defense plants and installations. Government today is the largest single employer in the West. This could be why westerners are apt to vote for liberal national candidates who can secure federal aid and for conservative local candidates.

Despite the decline of agriculture and mining, the lobbyists are still influential. The Cattlemen's Association is particularly powerful in Colorado and Wyoming, and the highly paid lawyers who represent the oil interests, utilities, and companies like Kennicott, American Smelting and Refining, and Anaconda are seen in the halls of every legislature. Education is well represented, too, because the westerner has been generous to his schools, and one of the greatest problems for sparsely populated states is how to finance education. Labor is not overly influential in Arizona or New Mexico; indeed, Arizona has a right to work law. In Colorado and Montana labor plays a larger role, but persists in fighting from the barricades of the nineteenth century. The Farmer's Union, which is considered socialistic by the corporations, has an active lobby. Conservation, a recent cause, is bound to attract more pressure groups in coming decades. Highways, liquor companies, merchants associations, taxpayers, bankers, real estate—their interests are predominately economic.

In some states lobbyists must register; in others it is not necessary. In Idaho, we are told, the corrupt-practices law permits evasion by lobbyists, while in Nevada lobbyists are regarded as friends and sources of information. In all the states the League of Women Voters, which lobbies for causes in which they are interested, is highly regarded for research on legislative matters. The League has done one of the most thorough studies to date on western water resources. In New Mexico the political scientists believe that lobbies are particularly effective because the state has a weak party system and lags behind other areas socially and economically.

Newspapers play an important part in shaping public opinion, perhaps more so than in other regions because television is nationally oriented, and while radio is heard on the most remote ranches, the papers are read for local and state news. Nearly every community has a small daily or weekly, and editions of the larger papers are distributed to rural as well as urban subscribers. Among the best known newspapers are the *Denver Post*, which might be described as conservative-moderate, but which, according to western tradition, has supported both Democratic and Republican candidates for national office. *The Arizona Republican* and the *Phoenix Gazette* are conservative in their outlook. Outstanding newspapers are those owned by the Lee chain of Iowa in Montana, once published by the Anaconda Company, which discouraged any criticism of the company or independent editorial thinking. Today these papers support local issues, give excellent coverage to state and national news, and print letters to the editor from concerned citizens.

Contrary to popular opinion, minority groups do not exert much political influence in the West. The Indians are not effective and show no evidence of becoming more so in the immediate future. The largest minority group, the Spanish-Americans, cannot be judged as a minority group in other parts of America. In the past the Spanish-Americans were a factor in the Southwest, particularly in New Mexico, but the influx of government employees, military and defense-plant workers, has altered the scene. Also, in New Mexico there was always a high degree of cultural assimilation and a strong civil rights tradition, as evidenced by past and present legislators and national representatives with Spanish-American names.

Even the Spanish-Americans and the Indians do not vote as a bloc and have traditionally belonged to both parties. This independence of the western voter has a disadvantage—it lessens what influence the West might have if it voted in a bloc, as did the South for so many decades. Also, it leads to a diminution of influence in the Democratic and Republican parties. What influence the West has is mostly in its individual representatives who have risen to positions of power because of their ability or because of seniority on congressional committees. Senator Mike Mansfield is an example of the former; Wayne Aspinwall, congressman from Colorado, is an example of the latter, who, because of his chairmanship of an Interior committee, has been able to block conservation measures that threatened oil interests.

Tom Paine of the University of Montana's Political Science Department feels that parties might become more important in the future. Certainly, there will be an increasing challenge between urban and rural interests, although many of the issues, such as finances, water, the environment, remain the same. Perhaps, the best definition of western politics is Mr. Paine's, "a tradition of no tradition."

Imitation Turquoise--
Tourism Brings
in the Dollars

X

"With a hearty handshake from the last frontier!"

Idaho welcomes the tourist to the western myth. Who cares if it is a commercial? It pleases the tourist and profits the westerner; make no mistake about it, the dollars are ringing in the tills. Income from tourism ranks first in Nevada, third in Wyoming, fourth in other states, and, in the approaching decades, promises to rank much higher.

Myth is tourism's greatest booster—the technicolor for the ad, the theme to the script. So thoroughly indoctrinated are Americans that the tourist accepts the myth without question. Some westerners even believe it themselves. They believe the myth of western hospitality, forgetting that tourism was slow to win recognition in a country that is one of the world's natural tourist areas. Indeed, tourism developed in spite of the westerner.

The tourist today is not necessarily from England or New York or Boston. He may be from Denver or Tucson or Seattle on a camping trip through Glacier Park, or he may have been raised in the West and is returning for a vacation. Conditions have changed since the nineteenth century, but touring the West today is still not the same as motoring through New England or doing a grand tour of Europe in a Volkswagen The land remains, and the distance and the attitude of westerners to tourists and of tourists to the West are unique to the region.

Do you remember *The Virginian*, a novel based on actual experience, where the newly arrived easterner asks if it would be possible to drive to the ranch by wagon that night and return later for his trunk? No, it would not be possible? Why? Because the ranch was 263 miles away.

No one approved of the easterner; it could have been because of his clothes, his accent, or his hat. And he, in turn, was too polite to comment on the dirty roller towel, the canned corned beef, the coffee with condensed milk, and the flies. The waitress did not put herself out and made no apologies for the food or accommodations. Take them or leave them, that's all there was.

The easterner symbolized the gentleman who did nothing and paid for service; he was, therefore, suspect in a country where every man worked whether he owned a ranch or dug ditches as a hired hand. Men were created equal, and service was not a privilege but an imposition.

The narrator of *The Virginian* would feel at home today in many cafés in small western towns or, indeed, in the large chain restaurants in Tucson or Boise. Here the corned beef has been replaced by hamburger and jello salad, and the waitress, reluctantly interrupting her chat with the cashier, demands of the tourist, "french fries or baked?" and brings a container of three glutinous dressings for a salad tossed from day-old leavings from the supermarket. The menu is always the same for dinner, steak, fried chicken, or prawns.

When we drive for more than two days through the West without a camper so we can do our own cooking, we buy milk, crackers, and cheese and have a picnic once a day.

This is not to say there are no good places in which to eat in the West. Mormon restaurants, if you can find them, do not serve liquor, but they do have homemade bread and real cream. Small, family-type Mexican places serve tostados with crisp crusts and sopapillas to dip in honey; some cafés with only counter stools serve real homemade huckleberry and cherry pie. Denver has two good, expensive restaurants; so does Colorado Springs. The food at dude ranches can be the real home variety lightened with salads and nonfattening desserts, but the best food and the cheapest is at Las Vegas where the gambling is expected to pay for the trimmings.

Bread, meat, and potatoes have been the western standby for generations—food that stayed with you, and it certainly did.

The West had no tradition of food and accommodations to appeal to the connoisseur. The Indians and the scenery made up for the inconvenience, and the tourist in the early days was more interested in survival than the niceties of life.

The ideal tourist, as far as the West was concerned, was also one of the earliest—Sir William Drummond Stewart, who had black hair, a beak of a nose, and rode a white horse to a rendezvous with the Rocky Mountain Fur Company brigades in 1833. Stewart could out-carouse, out-drink, and out-gamble Indians and trappers alike. He was so admired by the fur traders that he was declared to have in him the "hair of the black b'ar." According to one trapper he was generous with his money, "but what he wanted out thar in the mountains, I never just rightly knowed."

What Stewart wanted, and found, was the independence of the trapper's life, relationships founded on a perilous existence, the pride in survival, and courage and solitude in what was truly a Garden of Eden. In Stewart's experience we see the beginning of the western myth, for which ever after men were to seek in vain. Stewart's West did not long endure.

Frederick Ruxton, another English tourist, saw the early West, but he lacked Stewart's romantic vision. Ruxton was the dogged type, determined to tour the West, which in the 1840s often meant at the cost of life and health.

Ruxton wrote about his journey across the mountains. At the beginning of the pass, "the snow was of such a depth that the mules could hardly make their way to the top. Leading my horse by the bridle, I led the way, and at length, numbed with cold, I reached the summit . . . a blast struck me, carrying with it a perfect avalanche of snow and sleet, full in my front, and knocked me clean off my legs . . . . The animals strove in vain to face the storm, and turning their sterns to the wind, shrank into themselves, trembling with cold . . . . To remain where we were was certain death . . . there was nothing to do but reach the bottom as fast as possible, as it was nearly dark . . . . Before we had proceeded many paces from the edge of the plateau, horses, mules, etc., were rolling down the mountain all together and were at last brought up in a snow drift twelve feet deep . . . before a mule would stir, every pack had to be removed; and this, with a temperature some ten degrees below zero. I had to beat a road for the animals, by throwing myself bodily on the snow and pounding it down with my weight."

Ruxton had many remarks to make about the West,

among them the observation that coffee seemed to be the universal beverage; the other comment the advice to travelers given him by an old trapper, "Keep your primin' dry and your eye skinned."

The Indians, outlaws, and wild animals that inspired this advice are gone. Travel in the West, despite the long, uninhabited miles, is safer than in a city—perhaps, because the miles are uninhabited. If there are dangers, they are what they have always been, with regard to the land—no water in the deserts and snow in the high country. Every year hunters are lost and have to be found by sheriffs' search and rescue units. Recently, five boys attempted to climb a mountain in Glacier Park in January; their bodies have not yet been found. Last year an elderly couple from California, touring Wyoming, decided to explore an abandoned logging road. They high-centered on a rock and were sitting there, not at all worried when a hunter appeared.

"We knew someone would be by," they declared smiling.

The hunter could only stare. The last time anyone had been "by" was two years ago.

Francis Parkman represented another type of tourist, the scholar and historian. Parkman was inclined to be waspish in his comments about emigrants and inclined to be shocked by the lusty jokes of the Indians, but he could be excused; he had dysentery that kept him awake, and in addition to that, wolves howled all night and the horses kept tramping in and out among the tents in his camp on the Arkansas River.

The wonder is that, considering the difficulties, anyone toured the West. The reason, of course, was that myth drew tourists as it does now: adventurers, scholars, scientists, painters, people in search of health. Still, by modern standards the numbers of tourists were small. In the 1890s and as late as the first three decades of the twentieth century, touring the West was like touring Europe; it was limited to those who could afford it, and as a result, transportation and accommodations—while not as extensive as today—were more elaborate than they had been before or have been since. Who can forget the luxury of a stateroom on the Santa Fe Chief, paneled in rare woods, the seats upholstered in green plush, the private bath with the tiny metal bowl, and the dining car where you were seated by a steward at a table ornamented with monogrammed silver and a vase of fresh roses? The menu listed gourmet dishes, and at the end of the meal a white-coated waiter gave you a finger bowl. This was the period of the big lodges in the national parks, such as El Tovar in the Grand Canyon operated by Fred Harvey Company, which has been in the tourist business in the Southwest since 1876. Old Faithful in Yellowstone, the Sheridan Inn in Sheridan, Wyoming, the Utah Hotel in Salt Lake City, the Broadmore in Colorado Springs, the Alvarado in Albuquerque—these places were built for people who traveled by railroad, and some of them, like the Sheridan Inn and the Alvarado, were built on the railroad tracks.

By this time westerners were beginning to be aware of easterners who would pay to see the "real West." Until now westerners had been so busy building railroads, stringing fences, digging gold, plowing, and fighting Indians that they could not imagine the potentials of leisure. To the hard-working cowboy, the idle, able-bodied man was an object of suspicion, particularly if he spoke differently, dressed differently, and did not know which side of a horse to get on. The terms applied to easterners were derogatory—"pilgrims," "greenhorns," "dudes." And various indignities were visited upon them. Charlie Russell, the western artist, depicted a bunch of cowboys shooting at the feet of a gentleman in tweed knickers and eyeglasses to make him "dance." Taking a "dude" snipe hunting was another trick, as was putting a burr under his horse's saddle blanket so the beast would buck him off. These so-called practical jokes occasioned great hilarity; the easterners, for the most part, bore them good humoredly and, surprisingly, came back for more.

Dude ranches had their beginning in the still opulent days of tourism. One of the first ranches was the Eaton Brothers Ranch in Wyoming. Guests were carefully selected, for the atmosphere on a ranch was that of a large family. Operating a dude ranch became a socially accepted career, although old-time cowboys declared they would rather herd sheep than dudes. During the depression thirties many dude ranches had a difficult time financially—as did the railroads and big lodges. After World War II all but the hardiest went out of business due to high operating costs and the scarcity of help. Today many guest ranches have housekeeping cabins.

Perpetuation of the myth is important to dude ranchers, and fortunate, indeed, is the rancher when reality cooperates with myth. This happened to us one time on our ranch when my brother took an elderly gentleman from Boston for a wagon ride and suddenly found himself facing half a dozen men who materialized from a willow thicket.

"Throw down them reins and put up your hands!"

The order came from a fellow with a sheriff's star on his shirt. George, fearing the elderly gentleman might have a heart attack, hastened to inform the sheriff who he was; whereupon the sheriff explained he was looking for an escaped robber and had thought George might be the criminal. When George whipped the team home at a gallop to relate his adventure, we were delighted. What a story for the elderly gentleman—who suffered no ill-effects—to tell to his friends in Boston! In our wildest dreams we could not have asked for better advertising!

At dinner that evening we begged our guest to describe the exciting event. "Well," he said calmly, "I hate to say anything about it; things like that must be everyday occurrences to you."

Since World War II and the proliferation of the automobile and paved highways, perpetuation of the myth has become big business for chambers of commerce, state tourist bureaus, western wear manufacturers, the federal government, the Indians, rodeo associations, dude ranchers, packers, sporting goods stores, and horse breeders. The ski associations operate on myth, too, but not the myth of the Old West.

Western vacations today are not limited to the few who can afford them, they are available to anyone. As the publicists well know, the most satisfactory aspect of the West is that it can be graded for family consumption. It offers outdoor vacations, healthy activities, and all-American scenery. Even Las Vegas provides pastimes for kiddies. Campers and trailers have made it possible for families to travel as cheaply as it would be to stay at home. With this in mind, the national parks, the Forest Service, and private entrepreneurs have established campgrounds with toilet facilities, water taps, and outdoor fireplaces. In the summer the campgrounds look as though a general mobilization order had gone out to all American families with small, noisy children, but no one seems to mind the confusion. As a woman in Colorado said to me above the blare of transistors and screeches from a nearby swimming hole, "You get to meet such interesting people."

In the Southwest you can tell when winter is coming to other parts of the country by the number of trailers on the highway with out-of-state licenses. In the summer the trailers move north on the new interstates. Every year more country roads that lead off the interstates are improved; for the private car is the most popular mode of conveyance, despite airlines, buses, and trains.

Trains, today, are a sad relic of what they used to be. While European and Japanese railroads are developing fast, comfortable trains, our railroads are concentrating on freight, not passengers. Last month I traveled half a day on a once proud train. The seats were small and cheaply constructed. Small children screamed up and down the aisle with paper cups of soft drinks. The floors were covered with cheap, scrubbable linoleum. A pillow? After an hour's wait a surly porter brought me a tiny square demanding, "Seventy-five cents." Eating was cafeteria style, sandwiches and cokes and coffee.

The airlines are most in demand in the winter, because they offer quick transportation to the ski areas of Aspen or Sun Valley, where the beautiful people gather for sun on the snow and aprés-ski fun in Austrian-style chalets. Millions of dollars have gone into these ski areas so that they can compete with the European resorts. The heads of the ski schools are Austrian or Norwegian champions; the hotels serve croissants and café au lait for breakfast, and the boutiques stock Pucci blouses and Yves St. Laurent perfumes; yet none of the western ski resorts are as elegant as those in Europe. What college boy disguised in a white coat can compare to a Swiss-trained waiter who is proud of his profession? And it could be that the western myth is a handicap to elegance; Aspen may entertain the young, the beautiful, and the famous, but it was still the haunt of the old mountain man, tobacco-chewing Bill Williams.

Myth is more appropriate to Tucson, a tourist mecca despite the invasion of industry. In Tucson the season is winter. Before World War II many people came to the Southwest for health reasons, and they still do. At a party in Tucson

one evening, two-thirds of the guests told me they were win-
tering in Arizona because their doctors had told them the dry
air would be beneficial to their ailments. Still, the desert has
its own attractions, and the visitor who comes once is apt to
return, each time for a longer stay. The attraction of the
desert is difficult to define—the sun does not always shine,
and the dust storms can be annoying, so can the harshness of
the light. Why, then, do people find the desert so fascinating?
It could be because it has the stark simplicity of modern
sculpture. The colors are violent and explosive, sunsets burn
like crimson fires, and the mountains darken to purple silhouettes as the stars appear. In the Sonora Desert, where Tucson
is located, the colors are in light and shadow. Farther north in
the Painted Desert and in Bryce and Zion canyons in Utah,
the earth itself is stained terra cotta and geranium, violet and
vermillion. The country is as artificial as a stage setting, and
this encourages myth.

The script was not difficult to write, since the story had
already been told. Who could improve on the legends of lost
gold in the Superstition Mountains? or the padres like Father
Kino who established the missions? or the marauding
Apaches, the señoritas, the outlaws, and the silver lodes in
Tombstone?

The so-called ghost town of Tombstone lives on the
tourist trade. We saw it late in the afternoon when the long
shadows were falling across the treeless hills. In the town itself sunlight still warmed the restored façades of the Bird
Cage Theatre, the Crystal Palace Bar, and the livery stable
where Wyatt Earp and Doc Holliday shot it out with the bad
men. In season, the fight is re-enacted for the benefit of
tourists.

"It looks like a stage setting for a class-B western," a
friend observed.

"Yes," another agreed, "but why not? It shows you what it used to be."

The ghost towns are better restored by commercialization than allowed to decay into a heap of weathered timbers. The same applies to other mining camps in the West that have been rebuilt, such as Virginia City, Nevada, and Nevada City, Montana. Colorado has many old mining camps that are still inhabited—Cripple Creek, Leadville, and Central City. Scores of others have disappeared, leaving only a few mounds to mark the foundations of buildings. Some have been deserted for many years, and on what was once a street stands a cabin with a caved-in roof, a brick wall among the weeds, windows staring on emptiness, and the only sound, the wind.

Ghost towns are unique to the West, a subject for photographers and a goal for collectors of old bottles and for rock hounds who search the mine tailing for ore. If a tourist has an imagination, he will not need the publicists to tell him about the Old West, it is all around him.

The ghosts gather at Fort Garland in Colorado, too, where Kit Carson commanded, and that has been restored by the Colorado Historical Society; and at Fort Laramie, which is a National Historic Site administered by the National Park Service. This government department is to be commended on its program, although there is a tendency to spend more on comfort stations and parking areas than on preservation of the historical site. This, fortunately, is not the case with the Hubbel Trading Post on the Navajo Reservation, which is under federal control and has been left in its original state. Our last visit was on a spring morning when the earth, the leafless trees, and the adobe buildings all seemed the same sepia color against an intense blue sky. Inside, a tall, handsome Navajo man, wearing his hair clubbed in the old style beneath his high-crowned black hat, was discussing a loan on a silver and turquoise belt with the clerk who spoke to him in his own tongue. Behind the Navajo man stood his wife and daughter. Indian paintings hung on the wall along with woven baskets, and a glass case contained bracelets, earrings, and rings for sale. In the adjoining room finely woven rugs were heaped on the floors. Adjoining the trading post was the Hubbel home filled with rugs, baskets, and paintings. In one bedroom was a brass bed where Theodore Roosevelt slept when he visited the Hubbels. The home is open for tours, but commercialization has been kept to such a minimum that the visitor is not conscious of being an intruder.

The Navajos, like a number of other southwestern tribes, took advantage of the tourist boom in the 1960s and have planned for a continued boom in the next decades. The tribe owns Monument Valley, and the B.I.A. office at Window Rock arranged for a tour for me with the Golden Sands Tour Company. My guide knew the valley well; he also knew that as a native westerner and ex-dude rancher, I was aware that the Indian woman in a purple velveteen blouse weaving a rug in a freshly constructed hogan was there for the benefit of tourists; so was the little girl herding white sheep on a cinnamon-colored sand dune, but what did it matter? The scene was charming and showed how the Navajos had lived at one time.

The dancers at San Ildefonso near Santa Fe and at Walpi on the Hopi reservation dance for the benefit of tourists. This commercialization does not matter either. Walpi is one of the oldest inhabited villages in North America, a cluster of flat-roofed adobes clinging like swallows' nests to the mesa hundreds of feet above the desert. A woman in an open doorway cried, "Doll? You want to buy kachina doll?" and turned petulant when I shook my head. The young girls wore slacks and the older women wore tennis shoes, but the dancers in their kachina masks were from another era. The commercial touches were forgotten in the tinkling of bells and the rattling of gourds in the plaza high above the bone-grey desert.

Historical sites and Indian dances are apt to be considered dull by some people who want to be where the action is. In this case they should not come west at all, but should go to California.

Certainly the action is not at the older hotels that manage to retain the individuality of the opulent age of tourism. These older hostelries include La Fonda in Santa Fe, with its tiled floor, fireplace, and lobby where the Indians display silver and turquoise jewelry; the Strater in Durango, Colorado, which has been restored with the red plush and mahogany of the 1890s; the big lodges in the national parks that are still operating, such as El Tovar at Grand Canyon, built of rock and logs; and Old Faithful Inn in Yellowstone. These lodges have immense lobbies with stone fireplaces where you can sit in oversize chairs and watch the other guests or linger over the glass cases heaped with Navajo jewelry, post cards, and kachina dolls. The old hotels are growing shabby, and the bathroom fixtures are not the latest, but these hotels represent the Old West far more than do the chain-operated motels that stand, shiny and new as electric appliances, just off the Interstate and that have been furnished on an assembly-line basis with wall-to-wall carpeting, color TV, and chrome in the bathroom. These motels are built for the traveler who speeds through the West as quickly and superficially as he can. The other morning I woke up in such a motel, and as I gazed at the standard shelf built against the wall, ornamented with the standard mirror and the standard oversize lamp, I could not remember if I was in Reno, Nevada, or Portland, Oregon. Disturbed, I got up to look out the window and saw what I would have seen anywhere else—a swimming pool and, beyond the pool, a parking lot.

Air conditioning is essential and, if you have an air-conditioned car, it is possible to tour the West and take a breath of fresh air only when you step from the car to your motel or to a café.

Still it does not do to be too critical; for distances are long in Nevada and Wyoming, and many times we have been glad to see a "Vacancy" in neon tubes shining in the dusk. Before World War II the majority of accommodations in the West were limited to commercial hotels, whose front windows were ornamented with geranium plants in tin cans.

The new motels do not emphasize the western myth which is due to the influence of southern California that is sweeping in a technicolor cloud across the West. Californians do not care if Indians and cowboys still ride the Rockies. What Californians want are chain-store supermarkets with lots of parking space, used-car lots festooned with orange plastic flags, and franchised drive-ins selling burgers, tacos, and Tastee Freeze. Las Vegas is popular with Californians because it represents the epitome of this culture, particularly Caesar's Palace ornamented by pseudo-Greek statuary and fountains illuminated by colored lights. Las Vegas also has a convention center that seats thousands and the "Strip" where the sun never sets on the gambling casinos and hotels. Showsville, U.S.A., is the way they like to advertise it. Howard Hughes' Sands and the Desert Inn. Concrete and glass and neon signs and imported palm trees. The Tropicana has an eighteen-hole golf course, a theatre-restaurant, and a Folies Bergère. Visit the Fun Places owned by the Del Webb Corporation—the Sahara and the Thunderbird, where you can have free ice with the drinks in your room. See the Flamingo; the Dunes, which has the Casino de Paris Revue. See the

Wonderful World of Burlesque; Arturo Romero and his Magic Violins in the Sultans Stables; Frank Sinatra, Sammy Davis, the Supremes; the swimming pools in "lush tropical" surroundings. All this, a stage setting for the vast, dim arenas where daylight never penetrates and where women with platinum hair and tight pink slacks yank at the handles of slot machines and balding men in sport shirts stretched over bulging paunches shout, "Come again, baby!" at the crap tables. Blacks, Chinese, teachers on vacation, car dealers at a convention, salesmen, middle-aged wives in mink stoles and skirts that dip beneath their girdles, bare-bosomed show girls, and hard-eyed men in Hollywood style suits—the Mafia or professional gamblers?—they all are here.

I won a $7.50 jackpot on a nickel slot machine. A young man materialized, wrote down on a clipboard the number of the machine and the time it had disgorged the jackpot, handed me $5 (the remainder in nickels was heaped in the trough of the machine), and said, "Put in another nickel to clear the machine." To the young man, I was only a slot-machine number. Immediately, he moved to another customer in the racketing jungle of mechanical monsters.

In Las Vegas there is no foreign language to cope with, no Great Masters to stare at, obedient to a guide book. Forget the payments on the house, the doctor's caution about overdoing at your age. Las Vegas is the Sodom and Gomorrah of middle-aged, middle-class America. It does not cater to the western myth, but it carries on the tradition in a different way to a different type of customer. And who knows, in half a century Las Vegas may become a myth in its own right.

The easiest of all the myths to popularize is that of the cowboy. He has become big business supported by the Rodeo Association, western wear manufacturers, horse breeders, and magazines like *Hoofs and Horns* and *Western Horseman*, which is one of the best selling monthlies in the West and is read by thousands of men, women, and youngsters as soon as it appears. In times past the cowboy was a forty-five-dollar-a-month hired hand; now he belongs to a union and drives from rodeo to rodeo in a cream-colored car hauling a cream-colored horsetrailer. He might even fly his own plane. In the summer he contests in the north, and in the winter he goes south to the shows. There are schools for roping, cutting, and bronc riding, and a good roping or cutting horse is worth thousands of dollars. Quarter horses are preferred, but all western breeds—the pinto, the palomino, the appaloosa, and the mustang—appear in the arenas at one time or another and each has its supporters who claim unexcelled virtues. The appaloosa is supposed to be the intelligent, tough animal developed by the Nez Percé Indians; the mustang is a descendant of the mounts of the Conquistadores. If you want to hear legend magnified to epic proportions, listen to a group of horsemen.

Rodeo is the most typical western sport, an outgrowth of the cowboys' contests for fun in the early days of the range. Because rodeos are seldom seen outside the West, except at Madison Square Garden and in California, the tourists do not seem to mind the commercialization. The cowboys are young, indigenous to the West, and they wear their big hats cocked at an angle and walk stiff-legged in their high-heeled boots. In every performance they risk a crippling injury. I saw a bronc fall over backward and crush a man's chest. That adds to the thrill, too, for people in the grandstands are the same sort who watch for crashes in the auto races.

Rodeos are distinctive—hot sun, dust, plunging animals, and the cry, "Coming out of chute number four!" A rodeo is a great show and it's a pity that it has not had a Hemingway to create an international cult, but the western myth has never acquired social status.

What remains of the "real" West exists where it is least expected, and if the tourist is not observant, he will pass it by. This is the West of isolated cattle, sheep ranches, and the independent individual personified by the packer in the wilderness areas. It is not Kanab, Utah, where so many films have been made because of the cinnamon-colored cliffs and canyons; it is not Santa Fe, which is becoming a film capital and is equally spectacular, although in a different way with vast distances of silver sage and piñon pine and Indian pueblos. The real West is found in all the western states on the side roads, where gas stations are miles apart, where the motels in the decaying little towns were built of wood in the thirties and have homemade curtains at the windows and linoleum on the floor, where you eat at the only café where everyone knows everyone else and hashed browns come with the breakfast eggs.

Douglas, Wyoming, is on a main highway, but it is still the real West, a shopping center for the ranches on the plains. There is nothing to see or do there, and tourists drive through as rapidly as possible, but it is a place where men wear high-heeled boots and big hats for working clothes.

The packers wear high-heeled boots, too; for they wrangle horses and mules when they take people into the wilderness areas to fish and hunt. Like the ranchers, the packers don't bother about myth; they don't have to. The cut-throat trout still take a fly in the cold waters of the San Juans of Colorado and the Bitterroot-Selway of Idaho. The guest, lying in his sleeping bag beneath the stars, can sense his loneliness among the mountains as did the trapper of a hundred years ago.

The same feeling of isolation can be experienced on a float trip on rivers like the Colorado, the Green, or the Snake.

Most people make the trip with experienced guides in Navy life rafts—recommended for all but the most experienced. Last summer a party of us ventured the Salmon on our own. We had floated rivers before and were confident that we could do the River of No Return that flows through the second deepest gorge on the continent in the wilderness of central Idaho. Never shall I forget standing on the bank with a friend looking at the white water boiling over rocks, the thunder in our ears, knowing that in a few minutes we would have to brave that maelstrom in our tiny, two-man rubber boats. "I think," my friend said, "that I'm going to be sick to my stomach." As the Forest Service information sheet said, the amateur should remember that chances of rescue in case of upset were poor.

River floating is a new sport to the West, although not a new method of transportation, for the fur traders and explorers used the rivers as highways. The thrill and seeing parts of the country that cannot be seen otherwise are sufficient to attract the tourist without glamorizing river boating. Anyhow, the river boat men are a new and different breed from the cowboy, and it could be that they know that myth is not important—that myth is only the gilt on the genuine article. The tourists know this, too, as does anyone who stands on the rim of the Grand Canyon, or watches the geysers shoot skyward in Yellowstone, or walks at sunset on the rose-red dunes in Colorado or along the dead shores of the Great Salt Lake. Indeed, a man could wander a lifetime in the West and never cease to wonder.

Carmen in the Cow Camps

XI

On a recent visit to San Francisco, I was told by a friend, "You should see the Repertory Theater's production of *The Glass Menagerie*; then, you can go back to Montana and tell people you've seen a stage play."

The friend was well intentioned, so I did not tell her that the same play had been produced the previous year in our town by a competent cast from our own repertory theater and that a Broadway actress had acted the lead. In addition, the tickets had cost two dollars instead of ten dollars, and we arrived without fighting traffic at the theater ten minutes after we left our house.

Westerners are accustomed to being thought of as cul-

171

turally deprived.

As yet, we've seen no productions cast in the nude, but that does not mean that such entertainments are new to the West. Old-timers smirk over memories of shows in the honky-tonks of countless railroad towns and mining camps. Producers knew how to publicize them, too. What better "come-on" than the girls who met the train at construction towns naked except for a gossamer wrap?

But in the West nudity is not equated with art. The girls in the honky-tonks and the larger-than-life portraits of ample-bosomed females, which hung behind every bar with "Custer's Last Stand," saw to that. The West is too far from Broadway and too close to the honky-tonks for *Hair*.

This does not mean, however, that the West is a cultural wasteland. Indeed, the arts are flourishing as never before, due to affluence in the last two decades and government grants. State arts councils, universities, private donors, and the National Foundation on the Arts and Humanities have contributed money. So, too, has the Federation of Rocky Mountains States. Culture, westerners have discovered with some surprise, aids economic development. They were even told so by a Secretary of Commerce, who spoke at the Governors Conference in Denver in 1967.

"The nature and character of the local community and local government can have a significant impact on the prospects for growth. What is the intellectual climate of the community? Are there cultural opportunities in the area? . . . In those regions of the country which are flourishing, these conditions generally are favorable."

This speech convinced the chambers of commerce that they had better support the arts, and from then on businessmen contributed to the Symphony, as well as to the Community Chest and the local ball team. Their generosity, however, did not mean they became connoisseurs of classical music. One contractor, noted for his hard-drinking profanity, gave twenty-five dollars when I approached him for a donation.

"Are you coming to the first performance?"

"Christ, no! When I wanta hear music, I drop a nickel in the jukebox."

The universities are the centers for cultural activity, largely because they have the funds, the scholars, and the facilities. Their encouragement extends to the well-established cultural cities of Santa Fe and Aspen and to such isolated— and unexpectedly culturally concerned—towns as Hobbs, New Mexico, and Cody, Wyoming. Simultaneously, California illuminates the Rocky Mountains in living color, exciting and innovative. The same influence also results in commercialization, like black velvet pillows painted with giant cactus.

In the West what is popularly called culture is, like politics and the economy, in a process of change. A factor in the change is the turning of the Rocky Mountain region from the East to the West, a phenomenon of which, I suspect, the East is not yet aware.

When I was a girl, I was taken to New York to see the Metropolitan Museum and to hear the opera, and I was encouraged to read Tennyson and Dickens. Before my time the same English writers were read by literary groups in the mining camps, and the famous artists who played in our town (a convenient one-night stop on a transcontinental railroad) were from New York or Europe. Among the artists were Nordica, a singer who traveled in a private car with her own chef, David Warfield, and Otis Skinner. Those were the days of the traveling troupes and stage productions. Our town, so I've been told, had a theater converted from a livery stable, and when a gentleman playing the ghost in *Hamlet* made his exit, he dropped through a trap door onto a manure pile.

Culture, we were given to understand, not only by easterners but by westerners as well, emanated from New York,
Europe, and possibly Boston.

This is not true today. Campus unrest and the hippies,
originating in California, have brought with them a revolution in the arts that is reflected in the West. Previously, Hollywood had eroded the predominance of the East, if not by
excellence, at least by widening the audience.

And this, too, has been a factor in the change. The cowboys, lumberjacks, miners, and people who lived miles from
the railroad seldom saw a play or heard a great singer, and
many of them did not read books. An astonishing number
could not read at all. My father told me about a lumberjack
who desperately wanted to read but who was too proud to
admit he could not. For hours he would sit with the only book
he could find, a Bible, pretending to scan the pages.

"How do you like it?" my father asked.

"Oh," the lumberjack said, "all right; it's like all books,
it has a happy ending."

Today improved communication and education, highways, television, planes, autos, and affluence have brought
the arts within reach of everyone. World War II provided the
impetus for mobility, and continued prosperity enabled people to visit the cities that are, traditionally, culture centers.

You might visit Casper on the arid Wyoming plateau or
Hobbs on the plains of southeastern New Mexico and be
surprised by the interest shown in painting, crafts, and music.

In Casper a Chamber of Commerce official explained
this interest by indicating the oil refineries, which could be
seen from the window. When we drove into the city, we had
seen oil wells pumping among the ochre-colored hills. In
Hobbs oil produces wealth, too. "People travel," the official
said, "they hear good music and see good paintings. You

should see some of the pictures that are hanging in homes, here, and not all are in homes; some are in museums or art galleries, donated by people who want the state to have an art collection we can be proud of."

"Wyoming," I said, "is fortunate to have the Cody Museum endowed by the Whitneys."

As a Montanan, I spoke enviously because my state had not attracted Eastern money for such a project, and more than one Montana treasure had been bought for the Cody Museum. Countless other paintings, manuscripts, sculptures, and Indian crafts had gone—not only from Montana but from all the Rocky Mountain states—to museums, galleries, and collectors in the East, in Texas, and in California. The West was plundered of its cultural heritage, not by conquering armies but by dollars.

These art treasures—the paintings of Indians, cowboys, and cavalrymen against vast landscapes—the journals of fur traders and prospectors were part of the western myth, which made them valuable.

Ironically, the cowboys, miners, and Indians personify the West, while the average citizen in Hobbs, New Mexico, or Casper, Wyoming, is dismissed as a fake. This ambiguous identity of the westerner plays an important part in the cultural instability of the Rocky Mountain region. Dramatists, writers, and painters do not know if they should don a big hat and high-heeled boots or, in the words of the California hippies, do their own thing. In the end the majority settle for what will bring the best rewards, and don the big hat. New York and Los Angeles want no cultural competition, and besides, the western myth has proved too profitable to abandon.

Another impetus to the arts has been the migration of artists and writers to the Rocky Mountain region. Some come for a short time; José Iturbi conducted the Albuquerque Symphony Orchestra; Bernard Malamud served on the staff of a writers conference at the University of Montana. Many come to live in the area, particularly the Southwest, where Spanish adobes against the purple and terra cotta of the desert inspire painters as well as writers. D. H. Lawrence lived in Taos, Georgia O'Keeffe paints in New Mexico, and Frank Lloyd Wright's "Taliesen West" is located in Phoenix.

In Taos on a cold spring day, we visited a gallery presided over by a middle-aged woman wearing a velveteen blouse and silver and turquoise jewelry—the favorite costume of the art-conscious in the Southwest. The pictures were good and represented modern art, the impressionists, the traditional. We lingered before an oil of Indians riding through a snowstorm, reminiscent of the paintings of E. A. Burbank that hang in the Hubbel Trading Post on the Navajo Reservation, and of the paintings of Charlie Russell and Frederic Remington. Only the wealthiest collector of the most well-endowed museum can afford Russells or Remingtons today. Who better depicted the western myth?

The question of identity is easier for members of the performing arts than it is for painters and writers. Here the western myth is not so important. New York remains the hub of the theatrical and musical world, and those who would be successful, write, act, and produce with that in mind. Experimental theater on Off-Off Broadway is concerned with today's urban problems, not the long-ago mirage of a frontier, but experimental theater must have a large population from which to draw. In the Rocky Mountain area there are not enough of the intellectuals, the avant-garde, or those who want to be included in the "in-group" to permit a La MaMa, like that which flourished in New York in the late sixties and 1970. Occasionally, an original experimental play is produced by a college drama group, but on the whole amateur and professional casts in the West prefer Chekhov, Arthur Miller, Shakespeare, Ibsen, Tennessee Williams, and Neil Simon.

At the University of Colorado at Boulder, a student lies on the grass memorizing lines,

> There is a tide in the affairs of men,
> Which, taken at the flood, leads on to fortune...

The University at Boulder stages a summer Shakespeare Festival, costumed, lit, and acted with professional skill. During July and August the lights dim in the warehouse near Flathead Lake as the Bigfork Players bring Noel Coward and Neil Simon to western Montana—to Taos and Ruidosa, New Mexico; to the San Juan Playhouse, where the audience sips coffee in the patio beneath the stars during intermissions; and to Tucson and Coeur d'Alene, Idaho, where spectators swim in the cool, pine-scented waters of the lake before the curtain goes up. Some summer stock companies are more capable than others, but few are amateurish; the companies are largely composed of young men and women who have been trained in university drama departments by instructors who gained their experience on Broadway and in Hollywood. The days are past when the performing arts were taught by spinster ladies who had fallen on hard times.

Richard James, the spectacled, balding 1970 director of the Montana Repertory Theater, explained what theater is attempting to do in the West. "Our aim," he said, "is to bring first-rate entertainment to our region by using talented people of this area who can perform work of a professional caliber."

The reviews of professional critics, the glamor of first nights might be lacking when the theater on tour plays in a high school gymnasium, but the appreciation of the audience is sincere, as letters indicate—"Thank you and God bless you!"

In a newly furnished office in what had once been the carriage house of a copper king's mansion, Mr. Wilbur West, Director of the Utah State Institute of Fine Arts in Salt Lake City, told us about his state's symphony orchestra. Mr. West was enthusiastic and personable, as are so many of the representatives on Rocky Mountain state development boards. Mr. West was proud that the symphony, conducted by Maurice Abravanel, had toured California that year and a few years previously had played at Carnegie Hall to enthusiastic reviews. Combining art and economy, the Governor and 300 Utahans accompanied the symphony to promote industrial development by exhibits and luncheons at the Waldorf.

For an encore the symphony played the pastoral from Leroy Robinson's oratorio, *The Book of Mormon*, as what might be called the sole exception to an otherwise classical program. Symphonies and string quartets, like dramatists, prefer to interpret the masters, leaving Indian music to be taped by anthropologists and cowboy tunes to be heard on the jukeboxes.

Perhaps, of all artists, the writer faces the greatest problem in establishing his identity. A few years ago I attended a writers' conference where a nationally known literary critic and author conducted a series of seminars. The gentleman who was urban oriented had come from an eastern city. Despite some time in the West, he seldom ventured out of his academic milieu. I don't know what he expected from the class. What he wanted were young, impressionable minds whose potentialities could be developed; what he got were middle-aged ladies who had taken up writing. Still, he could not help stimulating even this audience. With beard thrust forward, eyes flashing, he preached symbolism, sex, and guilt. Not all the ladies understood what he was talking about—they were shocked, yet fascinated.

What emerged, as far as I was concerned, was a grotesque parody of a man in his own urban, academic environment. The image that he presented of the present-day westerner was no closer to reality than the mythical cowboy whose love life was limited to kissing his horse.

Who, then, are the westerners that the writer should strive to portray? The manager of a chain store in a growing town? The rancher who is a college graduate, whose ranch is fully automated without a horse on the place? The geologist who has the latest technical equipment and a helicopter to carry him to remote areas, along with a chemical toilet and cold beer? The hard-rock miner who earns $12,000 a year and owns a ranch-style home? The woods worker who lives comfortably with his family in a mobile home? We might hesitate over the professor who preaches ecology in a mining-oriented community. Or the young men who boom the logging trucks down the narrow mountain roads. Today the confrontations are in the metropolitan cities, not in the West, and even if a writer did succeed in describing this region, his book would be tagged as a "western." It is far easier to accept the inevitable and go back to the mythical cowboy and the prospector who struck it rich in the glory days of the frontier. Like everyone else, the writer looks back with nostalgia on vanished youth.

This could explain the preoccupation of scholars with the West. Few regions have been so researched and written about as the Rocky Mountains. If the West excels, it does so in history. Her scholars have been not only meticulous but eloquent, as witnessed by such men as Bernard De Voto, Frederick Jackson Turner, and Walter Prescott Webb. The list is endless and could also include such writers as Wallace Stegner, who insists he is not an historian but who describes his boyhood and the Mormon trek in prose as limpid as mountain waters.

The Indian, alone, does not have to worry about his cultural identity. He knows who he is. He is indigenous to the West and has only to concentrate on an art that antedated Columbus in the southwestern pueblos. The primitive colors and the stylized forms satisfy the avant-garde and appease the traditionalists, not all of whom are aware that the Spanish taught weaving and silversmithing to the Navajos. The crafts that nineteenth-century missionaries tried to eradicate are now being encouraged by the Institute of American Indian Arts established by the Bureau of Indian Affairs in 1962—a hundred years late, but better late than never. The institute is located in Santa Fe, where young people from all tribes are taught drama, creative writing, ceramics, painting, metalworking, and weaving. Here we saw true originality in a mask of slab-constructed stoneware with painted glaze decoration and in an abstract sculpture that might immediately be recognized as a lecherous old owl, although it was no more than a cone of metal—welded and brazed iron, so I was told. And if it had been for sale, and if I had been able to afford it, I certainly would have bought a bracelet of silver inlaid with slabs of turquoise and coral, which had been made by a Zuni boy from New Mexico.

To an assistant director of the Institute, I said, "What about creative writing?"

"You might like to read this," said the assistant director who gave me a publication of the Institute, pointing to a poem by a Navajo boy.

> I am the child of Yei-ie.
> Turquoise for my body. Silver for my soul.
> I was united with beauty all around me . . .

As brothers, the clouds are our long and sleek hair . . .
As brothers, the rivers are our blood . . .
As brothers, the universe is our home, and
in it we walk with beauty in our minds,
with beauty in our hearts and with
beauty in our steps . . .

When we left the adobe buildings of the Institute, I wondered if the great books, the great music, the great art of the future West would come from the Indians? What a source of untapped emotion and talent!

Much depends on continued support of the arts, not only for the Indians but every branch of the arts in the coming decades. The painting, the music, the drama, and the literature that is flourishing in the seventies could suffer from a cut in government grants; a decline in public support for the symphonies, the plays, and the art galleries would mean an end to many projects.

The West is already handicapped by a talent drain of artists who have left for New York and the West Coast, especially in the performing arts, but evident in other branches of the arts too. A sculptor friend, who does bronzes of cowboys, Indians, and buffalos, told me, when I remarked wistfully that I wished I could afford one of his pieces, "If you'd wanted to buy one two years ago, you could have had one for less than $200 but now I've an agent in New York who arranged to display my things at the Hammer Galleries, and I'm getting $2,000 for a single, small sculpture."

Dramatists and writers are told it is a waste of time to write television scripts—the center for television is in New York. Book publishers are in the East, too. So are musical comedy producers and the opera.

Once I was helping with a horse show, and a young man

sat beside me in the judge's section. He had black hair and a likable snub nose; I knew he was from Sand Point, Idaho.

"I have to sing the 'Star Spangled Banner' to open the show," he told me, "and I'm so nervous."

"Don't let it worry you," I assured him tolerantly, "just open your mouth and sing; the organ will be loud enough to cover any sour notes."

The young man stood up; the audience rose and the young man began our national anthem, his voice soaring above the organ, filling the huge auditorium with glorious sound. Today the young man is with the Metropolitan.

Fame and fortune are in New York and the West Coast, not in the Rocky Mountains. This fact presents another danger, especially in the universities, where the subject matter of the arts and the technique of presenting it are done with more concern to what is currently popular in New York, rather than what is indigenous to the West. Many intellectuals in the West, as well as the East, scorn the West as outmoded and no longer relevant.

What talent remains is frequently commercialized. Metal reproductions of the Navajo silver and turquoise jewelry are made in Hong Kong. A mail-order firm sells dyed chicken feather and imitation buckskin for costume kits. Records and rock groups parody the songs sung by cowboys driving the trail herds north from Texas. Literature has been so long cheapened by the shoot-'em-up pulps that the writers and the general public take it for granted, while service stations pass out Charlie Russell prints with each ten gallons of gas.

Still, the West can always hope that the Navajo boy will write more poems and that the Utah Symphony will one day perform a great opus composed by a native son.

And, Still, the Land

XII

On a north-south highway in Wyoming, a flagman waved a disk lettered in red, Stop! Ahead dust camouflaged earth-moving machines that rumbled like yellow mastodons across the earth. On both sides of the highway, the plains dwindled to the horizon, drab and cold in the wind that never stopped blowing. In the rear view mirror I saw a Cadillac with an out-of-state license nosing our bumper, at the wheel was a woman with champagne-colored hair and dark glasses that engulfed her features. The man in the seat beside her wore dark glasses, too. The car window lowered at the touch of a button, and the woman leaned out to the flagman—who was a bony fellow, aerosoled with earth from his tin hat to his jeans.

183

"How long do we have to wait?"

" 'Till I get the signal to let you through, Ma'am."

Manicured fingers tapped the wheel. "Is there anywhere around here we can get a cup of coffee or a drink? That road, where does it go?" The woman pointed to the road taken by a gravel truck that disappeared into the sagebrush.

"That goes to the Anderson ranch, ma'am, about thirty miles from here."

"My God, how can people live in such a country!"

The flagman looked at the woman. "Ma'am, I live in this country and I wouldn't exchange one foot of it for the whole city of New York or Los Angeles!"

Many westerners share the feelings of the flagman. Why? the urban oriented wonder—and with good reason— when they look at the plains of eastern Montana, Wyoming, and Colorado swept by bitter winds in the winter and scorched by the sun in summer. They look at the naked rock and deserts of Nevada, Utah, and the Southwest. They think of the high country of Idaho, Montana, and Colorado where the snow crusts until June. They drive through the towns that appear in capital letters on the maps to find the elevation figures higher than the population, and they wonder, as did the woman in the Cadillac, how people can live there. What do they do?

They see a couple of men gathered around a combination garage and gas station. The building is of wood; the paint is peeling and there is only one gas pump. The men turn to look at the car as it goes by. Watching tourists helps to pass the time, although traffic has diminished since the Interstate was built. Down the street is a grocery store. It is of wood, too, and in the window is a hand-lettered poster advertising last fall's Harvest Festival in the high school auditorium. The café next door to the grocery looks as though it were closed, but the middle-aged woman who owns it will serve coffee and a slice of pie, reflected upside down by mirrors in a glass case. The pie is stale. Most of the inhabitants appear to be either very young or very old. The women wear dresses from a nationwide chain store, and their hair is home permanented. High school girls, eyes caked with mascara and jeans pasted to their little buttocks, giggle on the corner. A rancher in a nylon-quilted jacket and wide-brimmed hat carries a fifty-pound sack of calf manna to his truck. Worry tightens the muscles about his mouth. In front of the town's single bar, a teen-age boy lounges, smoking a cigarette. The bar has a false front, and in its murky interior a neon sign advertises a popular beer. There is nothing for the boy to do but smoke and drink beer. No jobs are available and his friends are in high school or they have left town. In a while the boy will jump into his battered sedan and roar down the Interstate, and, someday, he will not come back.

The small, rural towns in the Rocky Mountain West, with few exceptions, do not resemble the towns in western television serials. They never did. Owen Wister in *The Virginian* described a Wyoming town that was typical of others on the frontier, "stark, dotted over a planet of treeless dust . . . Houses, empty bottles, and garbage, they were forever of the same shapeless pattern." But there is more than decay and isolation. The West, like any region, demands understanding.

Not long ago a New York writer came west to write about Utah. In his article for a national magazine, he indicated that the Mormons were ultraconservative. What really appalled him was that there were no bars in Utah and an out-of-state couple could not (imagine) buy wine in Kanab! What was worse, there was little to do in the state but hunt and fish. These observations were gathered during a brief stay in Salt

Lake City and a trip on the Interstate in an air-conditioned car.

Westerners do not appreciate such ignorance. Nor do they appreciate well-known comics who say, "Missoula! I don't know where that is, but it sounds like a salad oil!" or urban newspapers that like to print with humorous remarks weather reports that show Yuma, Arizona, as the hottest place in the nation and West Yellowstone as the coldest. And they do not appreciate remarks such as a friend made to me after a transcontinental flight, "I don't know why they're worried about the population explosion with all that open space in Nevada."

Personally, I feel that as cities have grown, the rural areas of America have become correspondingly remote, if for no more than physical reasons, and that improved communications do not bridge the gulf. The cities have developed their own problems, while rural America's problems have grown in a different direction. Politically, such an argument might be bolstered by citing as an example President Nixon's proposal in 1970 to accelerate the trend toward more state involvement in federally financed programs. The city administrations, fearing rural dominated legislatures, fought the proposal, preferring to have direct support from Washington for the poverty program, model cities, aid to education, and other programs that benefited the cities.

Primarily, the West remains a rural region and this is a disadvantage, for the politicians and economists point out that our society is no longer agricultural and that most Americans live in urban areas. In our drive for progress, the frontier that once inspired Americans has been devoured by our insatiable desire for raw materials and land. Now progress has moved to the cities, leaving the rancher, the small independent farmer, the businessman in the decaying towns, the cat skinner and the logger a minority in the nation.

But the economists forget those cities of no more than 2,500 in the West, just as they forget the proximity of the big cities to the open country. The West might be urban in population, but it is rural in much of its thinking.

The urban oriented do not see behind the façades of the wooden buildings in the small towns. They only see—as we all do—what they want to see, failing to comprehend the meaning of the mountains and the empty miles or the cities that are drawing people from the small towns. In these cities there is a new vitality. Today cowboys and Indians are not necessary to a frontier. Nor is a mad rush for gold or free land inspired by ignorance and rumor.

The West remains a frontier, but instead of the raw resources that were wrested from it in the past, today it offers space and the few remaining wilderness areas in a nation where these things are becoming scarce. Because these are difficult to evaluate, they are also difficult to comprehend. Economic opportunity is still the most acceptable reason for moving west, although it might not be the real one. The coal, the oil, the timber, and the water are tangible, the environment is not.

This does not mean that the western myth has vanished. The West will always be mythical. The geographical characteristics make that inevitable, and the human spirit withers without belief in the existence of some Utopia. Today the difference is in degree, and the utopia is somewhere away from cities that are growing uninhabitable and countrysides that have been developed into commercial horrors.

Yet the past is repeated in this way. The West is not a utopia now, any more than it was during the gold rush, and the modern emigrant in search of a favorable environment must expect to encounter difficulties.

First of all, much of the space in the West is uninhabitable under modern conditions. Miles of desert in Utah,

Arizona, and Nevada and the high plains of northern Montana are empty because they will not support a sizable population; these are the areas that have lost in the census; consequently, the more livable areas have gained in population, and land has gone up in price.

Living off the land, as many young people have tried to do in the tradition of the agrarian utopia, results only in disaster.

In the rural towns as well as in the cities, there is an increase in crime, smog, drugs, and all the problems of the big metropolitan areas. The only difference is in magnitude and in the fact that there is still time for people to fight and control the problems.

But they will receive little help from the old-time westerner. That character, as depicted by myth, is either an old man or dead. His identity depended on isolation and an economy that exploited natural resources. Today even the wilderness areas are not so remote that amenities such as outside toilets cannot be found; meanwhile, natural resources are nearing exhaustion or at least are no longer accessible to the individual.

In the Bitterroot-Selway Wilderness, which we packed into by horseback, the first thing we saw upon reaching camp after an all-day ride was a Cessna plane perched on a wild meadow. The plane was a disappointing symbol of civilization, but times had changed; we had adjusted to the fact and could even dispense with nostalgia and acknowledge that most of the change had been for the better. This was evident that day in the Bitterroot-Selway Wilderness. The plane's pilot, a lean young fellow in jeans and a wide-brimmed hat, was of the new breed in the West who have looked to the future but who have also carried on the tradition of daring and mastery of the land. A lady in our party exclaimed, "He's a backwoods Sky King!" What was more to the point, he was a modern westerner.

The packer, on the other hand, who was grey haired and quiet and had spent most of his life in the wilderness, represented the Old West. Men such as he are becoming scarce, and if they disappear altogether—indeed, as they are disappearing—their passing will not be noticed. For a long time they have had little impact on the economic and social life of the West.

Another modern westerner was a young rancher we met last summer. Jim Wood, who owned the V-X ranch near Sand Point, Idaho, symbolized hope for the small, independent rancher. We stayed at the Wood's place during a competitive trail ride; that is, we spread our bedrolls beneath the trees, but kept our horses in Wood's stout, new corrals and ate in the barn, whose floor was covered with freshly sprinkled sawdust. Jim Wood was young, had an attractive wife and five children, and earned a good living on his land, which he had cleared for hay and pasture. The barn had electric lights, the farm operation was fully mechanized, and Mrs. Wood had a washer, dryer, and television set in the house. In 1969 Jim Wood was awarded the title Grassman of the Year for Idaho, a title that is not easy to win. Like most ranchers today, Wood was educated, he spoke well, and he worked hard. So did his youngsters.

"Do you have much trouble with juvenile delinquency in the schools?" I asked.

"We have some," Jim admitted. "I guess everyplace does these days. Sand Point's close to Spokane; the kids go there and get into trouble. So far, we've had no trouble with our kids. They're too busy—4-H projects, the chores, fishing."

When we pulled the electrical connection loose on our horse trailer, Jim worked all afternoon to repair it, and, when we offered to pay him, he waved us aside; he was glad to help a friend.

Jim Wood is far removed from the violence and protest of the big cities. He might also be called by some culturally deprived, but if so, he has compensations. He has what many people are seeking today.

The hippies are another group that might be described as modern westerners. In the last few years, they have moved into the West by hitchhiking and in gayly colored buses; they settle in communities near a university or an art center, such as Taos, New Mexico. It was here on one cold spring day that we talked to two wispy-bearded boys in jeans.

"Yeah, we like it here. It's warm most of the year. We got a shack to live in, and we can get all the grass we want . . ."

The local townspeople, afraid that the hippies will discourage tourists, feel that the youths are new to the West. They forget that a hundred years ago many emigrants were misfits and rebels in a society from which they came and that some became citizens of whom the West was proud, while others became derelicts in construction towns.

The hippie culture has its merits in the present-day West. To a certain degree, the young people know what they are looking for. Stewart Brand of Menlo Park, photographer and promoter of an underground catalogue for the hip movement, explained:

". . . a lot of people are into the Western myth, you know, to build a town. They want to invent and discover things for themselves. But it takes margin to invent, and it's hard to invent in the cities . . . I think the thing we're talking about is no more or less hard to understand than the simple desire to have a home. A home and a sense of home that can only grow out of a sense of place. Cities aren't places anymore.''

This is also what the businessmen and the housewives in the western cities feel. The natives and the newcomers are adjusting to the new West. They are active in conservation and in civic affairs and are aware of local and national politics; what is more, they are ready to participate in whatever way they can to maintain the quality of the environment. No longer does the intelligent westerner want to exploit his environment, he wants to preserve it; while those who would exploit it are discovering that, by popular acclaim, they must learn to compromise. This is the basis for the new vitality.

I like to think that the Old West, which was not entirely bad, and the new West, which is not entirely bad either, will fuse into a future West—and this seems to be occurring. The tide is turning, as it did when the prospectors flooded back from the Sierras to the placer diggings in the Rockies. In this future West the frontier will no longer need to be exploited by myth, but will provide for Americans today, ''a home and a sense of home that can only grow out of a sense of place.''

Bibliographical Notes

It would be difficult to list all of the sources for this book since
the material includes personal experience and interviews of a
lifetime, as well as monographs, magazine articles, and newspaper items too numerous to name. Primary source material
was limited intentionally because this book is not a scholarly
or historical study, but a general commentary on the West by
a native westerner.

However, some sources might be of interest to the
reader. Of particular value on the geography of the West
were these books and pamphlets: John Wesley Powell, *Report
on the Lands of the Arid Region*, U.S. Geological Survey,
Washington, D.C., 1878; Jerome Wyckoff, *Our Changing*

Earth Through the Ages, Golden Press, New York, 1967; The
State Guide Books in the American Guide Series, such as
Montana, Viking Press, New York, 1939, and *Nevada*, Bin-
ford and Mort, Portland, 1940; Willard Johnson, *The High
Plains and Their Utilization;* the Twenty-first and Twenty-
second Annual Reports of the U.S. Geological Survey, Part
IV, Twenty-second Annual Report, Washington, D.C., 1902;
the booklets *Natural Resources* for all the western states, published by the U.S. Department of the Interior, Washington,
D.C.; *The Great Rivers of the West*, an excellent study by the
League of Women Voters of Idaho, Montana, Oregon, and
Washington, published by Koke-Chapman, Eugene, Oregon,
1959; state publications from all the western states that included such pamphlets as *New Mexico's Forest Resource*,
U.S. Forest Service, Ogden, Utah, and *Mosaic of New Mexico's Scenery, Rocks and History*, edited by Paige Christian-
sen, State Bureau of Mines and Mineral Resources, Socorro,
New Mexico, 1967.

Also of interest were Gloria Griffin Cline, *Exploring the
Great Basin*, Oklahoma Press, Norman, 1963; Wallace W.
Atwood, *The Rocky Mountains*, Vanguard Press, New York,
1945; Joseph Wood Krutch, *The Desert Year*, Viking Press,
New York, 1960; and Loren Eisley, *The Firmament of Time*,
Atheneum, New York, 1966.

More comprehensive books on the West are Walter Prescott Webb, *The Great Plains*, Grosset and Dunlap, New York,
1931; Robert G. Athearn, *High Country Empire*, University
of Nebraska Press, Lincoln, 1960; Wallace Stegner, *Beyond
the Hundredth Meridian*, Houghton-Mifflin, Boston, 1962;
Henry Nash Smith, *Virgin Land*, Random House, New York,
1950; Ross Toole, *Montana, an Uncommon Land*, University
of Oklahoma Press, Norman, 1959; Harold Briggs, *Frontiers
of the Northwest*, Appleton-Century, New York, 1940; How-

ard Lamar, *The Far Southwest, 1846-1912; A Territorial History*, Yale University Press, New Haven, 1966; Joseph Kinsey Howard, *Montana, High Wide and Handsome,* Yale University Press, New Haven, 1943; T. J. McCleneghan, *Land Ownership in the West,* University of Arizona Press, Tucson; Victor Westphall, *The Public Domain in New Mexico 1854-1891,* University of New Mexico Press, Albuquerque, 1965; Roy M. Robbins, *Our Landed Heritage,* University of Nebraska Press, Lincoln, 1962; LeRoy Hafen, *Colorado, the Story of a Western Commonwealth,* Peerless Publishing Company, Denver, 1933; Marshall Sprague, *The Great Gates,* Little Brown, Boston, 1964; Frederick Jackson Turner, *The Frontier in American History,* Henry Holt, New York, 1947; Miguel Antonio Otero, *My Life on the Frontier, Vol. II, 1882-1897,* University of New Mexico Press, Albuquerque, 1939; Walter Prescott Webb, *The Great Frontier,* Houghton-Mifflin, Boston, 1952; LeRoy and Ann Hafen, *Old Spanish Trail,* Arthur Clark Company, Glendale, California, 1954; Earle R. Forrest, *Missions and Pueblos of the Old Southwest,* Arthur Clark Company, Cleveland, 1929.

Among the many books on the westward migration, I found these helpful: *The Odyssey of Cabeza de Vaca,* Morris Bishop, Century Company, New York, 1933; John Charles Frémont, *Memoirs of My Life,* Belford Clark and Company, Chicago, 1887; Meriwether Lewis, *Journals of Lewis and Clark,* 1814 Edition Unabridged, J. B. Lippincott, Philadelphia, 1961; William H. Goetzmann, editor, *Army Exploration in the Far West,* Yale University Press, New Haven, 1959; Wallace Stegner, *The Gathering of Zion,* McGraw-Hill, New York, 1964; Dale Morgan, *The Humboldt, Highroad of the West,* Rinehart and Company, New York, 1943; Oscar Handlin, *The Uprooted,* Grosset and Dunlap, New York, 1951; Susan Shelby Magoffin, *Down the Santa Fe Trail and into*

Mexico, Yale University Press, New Haven, 1927; Reuben Gold Thwaites, Early Western Travel Series, extract from Josiah Gregg, *Commerce of the Prairies,* Arthur Clark Company, Cleveland, 1905; Bernard De Voto, *Across the Wide Missouri,* Eyre and Spottiswoode, London, 1948; also, De Voto, *The Course of Empire,* Houghton-Mifflin, Boston, 1952, and *The Year of Decision, 1846,* Little Brown, Boston, 1942; Albert Richardson, *Beyond the Mississippi,* American Publishing Company, Hartford, 1867; William Kelly, *Across the Rocky Mountains,* Sines and M'Intyre, 1852; Sara Raymond Herndon, *Days on the Road,* Burr Printing House, New York, 1902; Francis Parkman, *Journals,* edited by Mason Wade (two volumes), Harper and Brothers, New York, 1947; Robert Riegel, *America Moves West,* Henry Holt and Company, New York, 1956.

Selected from among the many books on the fur trade were Charles Larpenteur, *Forty Years a Fur Trader,* edited by Elliott Coues, Ross, and Haines, Minneapolis, 1962; John Work, *Journal,* edited by Paul Phillips, Arthur Clark, Cleveland, 1923; W. A. Ferris, *Life in the Rocky Mountains,* edited by Paul Phillips, Old West Publishing Company, Denver, 1940; Dale Morgan, *Jedediah Smith,* Bobbs-Merrill, Indianapolis, 1953; Robert G. Cleland, *Reckless Breed of Men,* Alfred Knopf, New York, 1950; George F. Weisel, *Men and Trade on the Northwest Frontier,* University of Montana Press, Missoula, 1955.

Material on the Indians is so voluminous that it was difficult to select these books from among the many: William Brophy and Sophie D. Aberle, *The Indian; America's Unfinished Business,* University of Oklahoma Press, Norman, 1966; George Hyde, *Red Cloud's Folk,* University of Oklahoma Press, Norman, 1937; Clark Wissler, *The American Indian,* Oxford University Press, New York, London, 1922; Robert W. Young, *The Role of the Navajo in the Southwestern*

Drama, Gallup Independent, Gallup, New Mexico, 1968; John C. Cremony, *Life Among the Apaches*, republished by Arizona Silhouettes, Tucson, Arizona, 1951; John P. Clum, *Apache Agent*, Houghton-Mifflin, Boston, 1936; John C. Ewers, *The Blackfeet*, University of Oklahoma Press, Norman, 1958; Vine Deloria, *Custer Died For Your Sins*, Macmillan Company, New York, 1969.

Indispensable to any study of the Indian are the bulletins published by the Bureau of American Ethnology, such as those on the Apache, the Navajo, and the Zuni, indeed, on all the western tribes. Equally informative, particularly on the Indian today, is *The White Mountain Apache Indians* published by the White Mountain Apache Tribal Council at Fort Apache, Arizona, 1958; *The American Indians and the Federal Government* published by the Bureau of Indian Affairs, Washington, D.C.; *The Navajo Yearbook, 1951-1961: a Decade of Progress, Report No. VIII*, published by the Bureau of Indian Affairs, Navajo Agency, Windown Rock, Arizona, 1961; *Tribal Governments and Law and Order*, State of Montana, Department of Indian Affairs, Helena; *The United States Indian Service*, Bureau of Indian Affairs, Washington, D.C.; *Southwestern Indian Tribes*, Tom Bahti, KC Publications, Flagstaff, Arizona, 1968.

The mining frontier offers these classics: Nathaniel P. Langford, *Vigilante Days and Ways*, J. G. Cupples Company, Boston, 1890; Granville Stuart, *Forty Years on the Frontier*, edited by Paul Phillips, Arthur Clark Company, Cleveland, 1925; *Copper Camp*, W. P. A. Writers Program, Hastings House, New York, 1945; Robert Brown, *An Empire of Silver*, Caxton, Caldwell, Idaho, 1965; Glenn Chesney Quiett, *Pay Dirt*, Appleton-Century, New York, 1936; Annie Ellis, *The Story of an Ordinary Woman*, Houghton-Mifflin, Boston, 1929.

Information on mining today was obtained from reports

such as the annual reports of the New Mexico Bureau of Mines and Mineral Resources at Socorro, New Mexico. The state bureaus of mines in all the western states put out such annual reports. Also helpful were the annual reports of the big companies such as Kinnecott, Anaconda, and American Smelting and Refining. The Valley National Bank in Phoenix, Arizona, publishes a monthly report of the Arizona economy that includes a report on mining activity in the state. The industrial development boards of all the western states publish information on mining. One such publication is the Utah Industrial Progress Report; another is *New Mexico, Profit Land, U.S.A. The World Almanac* published annually by the Salt Lake Tribune contains many pertinent figures with regard to mining activity in the West. So, too, does the *Book of Facts and Statistics and Information* published by the Department of Commerce, Washington, D.C. In addition, information on mining is available in pamphlets from the Geological Survey, Department of the Interior, Washington, D.C.

Two suspenseful accounts of early-day tourists in the West are Lewis Garrard's *Wah-To-Yah and the Taos Trail*, Oklahoma Press, 1955, and George F. Ruxton's *Adventures in Mexico and the Rocky Mountains*, John Murray, London, 1861.

Works on military campaigns on the frontier could comprise a library in itself. From the many journals, diaries, and studies, I chose: Robert G. Athearn, *William Tecumseh Sherman and the Settlement of the West*, University of Oklahoma Press, Norman, 1959; John Bourke, *On the Border with Crook*, Charles Scribners, New York, 1891; Virginia W. Johnson, *The Unregimented General*, Houghton-Mifflin, 1962; Don Rickey, Junior, *Forty Miles a Day on Beans and Hay*, University of Oklahoma Press, Norman, 1963.

The classic study for the cattle industry is Ernest Staples

Osgood's *Day of the Cattleman*, University of Minnesota Press, Minneapolis, 1929. Also, Walter Baron Richthofen, *Cattle Raising on the Plains of North America*, University of Oklahoma Press, Norman 1964; General James S. Brisbin, *The Beef Bonanza*, University of Oklahoma Press, Norman, 1959; Gene M. Gressley, *Bankers and Cattlemen*, Alfred Knopf, New York, 1966; John Rolfe Burroughs, *Where the Old West Stayed Young*, Bonanza Books, New York; John K. Rollinson, *Wyoming Cattle Trails*, Caxton, Caldwell, Idaho, 1948; Walt Coburn, *Pioneer Cattlemen in Montana*, University of Oklahoma Press, Norman, 1968.

References for the homestead days included Annie Pike Greenwood, *We Sagebrush Folks*, Appleton-Century, New York, 1934; Adelia Parke, *Memoirs of an Old Timer*, Signal American Printers, Weiser, Idaho, 1955; H. G. Merriam, editor, *Way Out West*, University of Oklahoma Press, Norman, 1969 References previously cited, such as Howard's *Montana* and his *High Wide and Handsome*, Robert Athearn's *High Country Empire*, and Henry Nash Smith's *Virgin Land* contain chapters on homesteading. Also two unpublished papers were of great help: Rufus Jones, "Joys and Sorrows of a Dry Land Ranch," a manuscript in the library of the University of Montana, and John H. Toole, "Montana Agriculture and the Federal Reserve Bank of Minneapolis, 1917-1925," a paper Mr. Toole prepared for delivery to a meeting of the Federal Reserve Ninth-District officers in Minneapolis in 1968.

A most informative book about the western economy was Harvey S. Perloff, Edgar S. Dunn, Eric Lampard, and Richard Muth's *Regions, Resources and Economic Growth*, University of Nebraska Press, Lincoln, 1967. Other books are Fred Shannon, *The Centennial Years; A Political and Economic History of America from the Late 1870's to the Early 1890's*, Doubleday and Company, Garden City, New York,

1969; Robert Edgar Riegel, *The Story of the Western Railroads*, University of Nebraska Press, Lincoln, 1967; *Resources for the Future*, Annual Report published by Resources for the Future, 1968, Washington, D.C. Also helpful were pamphlets and reports from the eight states, including the report of the *Rocky Mountain States Governors Conference to Accelerate the Regional Economic Growth By Broader Application of Science and Technology*, September 1967, published by the Area Development Department, Colorado Springs, Colorado. In addition, reports published by state industrial development boards are useful, such as *Nevada: Community Profiles*, which contains figures on transportation, population, employment, wage rates, resources, utilities, finances, and industry; reports such as the *Fourth Annual Business-Economic Outlook Forum* published by the Colorado Division of Commerce and Development, Denver, 1968; and reports of private utilities, such as Mountain States Telephone Company.

The most helpful reference for the chapter on politics was the volume edited by Frank H. Jonas, *Politics in the American West*, University of Utah Press, Salt Lake City, 1969. Other references for the chapter on western politics, as well as the chapters on arts and conservation, were derived to a great extent from state publications, professional journals, newspapers, and magazines.

On the subject of conservation, I read Raymond Dasman, *An Environment Fit for People*, Public Affairs Pamphlet Number 421, New York, 1968; *The Population Challenge*, United States Department of the Interior, Yearbook Number 2, Washington, D.C.; *A Ten Year Program of Federal Water Resources Research*, U.S. Government Printing Office, Washington, D.C., 1966, Office of Science and Technology. The publications on the environment are multiplying at a dizzying rate and would be too numerous to list here. So, too, would the magazines and newspapers used as references, but those I referred to most often might be named: the state historical publications, such as the *New Mexico Historical Review, Montana,* the *Magazine of History,* and the *Utah Historical Magazine.* The magazines published by the state highway departments were also frequently referred to. These include *Arizona, New Mexico, Nevada,* and other similar publications. The newspapers ranged from little-known weeklies, such as the *Navajo Times* and the *Mining Record* (the voice of the mining industry), to the papers that I read regularly, such as *The New York Times,* the *Daily Missoulian,* the *Denver Post,* and the *Salt Lake Tribune.*